Uruguay in Transition

Uruguay in Transition
From Civilian to Military Rule

Edy Kaufman

Transaction Books
New Brunswick, New Jersey

Copyright © 1979 by Transaction, Inc.
New Brunswick, New Jersey 08903

Library of Congress Catalog Number: 78-55939
ISBN: 0-87855-242-1 (cloth)
Printed in the United States of America

Library of Congress Cataloging in Publication Data
Kaufman, Edy.
    Uruguay in transition.

    Bibliography: p.
    Includes index.
    1. Uruguay—Politics and government—1973- 2. Uruguay—Politics and government—1904-1973. 3. Uruguay—Armed Forces—Political activity. I. Title.
F2729.K38   322'.5'09895   78-55939
ISBN 0-87855-242-1

Contents

List of Illustrations

Foreword

To my knowledge, this is the first book that covers the dramatic events of the 1970s in my country, Uruguay, where a deep-rooted democratic system was replaced by one of the most repressive regimes in Latin America. It is a pleasant duty to associate myself with Dr. Kaufman's endeavors to explain the different internal and external causes that brought about such an abrupt change. After discussing at length with the author about his interpretation of the political events in my country, I would like to add some brief comments of my own, with the aim of further clarifying some vital points: the meaning of what Dr. Kaufman calls *autogolpe* and President Bordaberry's responsibility in this event; the role played by the Congress, which I personally share in the process of the destruction of the democratic institutions in Uruguay; and the attitude of the people in my country facing such a dramatic development.

The expression *autogolpe* (self-coup) has been used as the antithesis of coup d'etat, by which the armed forces overthrow a civil regime. In the former, it is the government itself which uses force, namely, coercion is not utilized against it. The fact that the government later became trapped by the force that it originally unleashed was a possible outcome of such a process. However, I would not underestimate the responsibility of President Bordaberry and his advisers in the resulting coup. Although it is correct to underline that the intervention of the Uruguayan military in politics was a much longer process, I do not think that the military could have driven this road to the very end had Bordaberry himself not favoured it. He did not entirely oppose the idea of the coup from its incipient stages; as was shown at a later time, his personal ambitions were such that he indulged himself with the notion of dismantling the legislative power and emerging as a dictator. Such an antidemocratic bias was rooted both in his long-standing ideology and background. I believe that Bordaberry was conscious of his own mediocrity as a politician, a self-realization difficult to combine with his own vanity. He could not, therefore, ever forgive those people and institutions which provided clear evidence of his inferiority. He did not forget that his own election as president of Uruguay was due to technical circumstances, and that somebody else—Pacheco—was really

ix

the candidate of his own party. He took offense to the fact that other leaders enjoyed the popularity he was lacking. He hated Parliament because he was virtually unknown after many years in the Senate. He reacted against the political parties in Uruguay because he did not really belong to either of them. Although at a certain conjunction of time he did collaborate alternatively with the two traditional political parties, Bordaberry never felt connected to what these parties meant or stood for. Furthermore, his personal ideas were surely influenced by the close circle in which he associated, always linked to the most antidemocratic currents of opinion; sympathizing with the Nazis in his youth; admiring Franco, supporting the 1933 coup d'etat in Uruguay; and publicly defending the fascist group Juventud Uruguaya de Pie (Uruguay Youth Stand Up). For these reasons, it should not be surprising that his aim was to abolish, if possible, democracy in Uruguay.

The military and the president had to face, for such a purpose, the opposition of Parliament. Here is the place to comment on the opinion that the closer the expected coup came, the more erratically and inefficiently the political parties reacted. Although such a statement may seem to be true at first glance, one should not overlook the fact that the institutional system had only limited possibilities of defense. In a presidential regime, the role of the advocator of civil institutions is played mainly by the head of the executive branch, as it is explicitly stated in our Constitution. However, in the case under consideration, it was precisely the president who attempted to destroy the institutions. Not only did he forfeit his own powers, but he also raised himself as the banner of the mutiny. So what could the Parliament do, facing such a threat? Its weapon could have been to count on the honor of those monopolizing the use of force and ask for their support. In my opinion, the battle was lost when the military claimed that the capture of the Legislative Assembly was carried out under the orders of the commander in chief who, as stipulated by the Constitution, is the president himself. It is thus important not to misread the congressional documents of this period, in which the expressions of trust that the armed forces would not impede the constitutional order were later interpreted as evidence that the legislators failed to perceive the real magnitude of the threat. This was not the case. Such declarations were, in fact, appeals to the responsibility and the respect of the traditions of the country and the armed forces.

The Uruguayan Parliament, as all parliaments, was and is a viable institution, a reflection of the spirit of the nation. Taken as individuals, its members were no more than a group of common Uruguayans, having neither more nor less virtues and faults than the rest of their compatriots. But there are some historic moments in which simple human beings feel themselves inspired by an extraordinary force and serve the cause beyond their normal strength. I believe that this was the case with the Uruguayan Parliament. In the first stages, after failing to obtain an electoral majority, the government sought the support of

Parliament through distributions of positions in the administration and other bonuses. It found those who, in exchange for personal advantages, were ready to offer their votes. It is important to stress these points since it was often said that the government was faced with obstruction from a hostile Parliament. At the beginning, the president faced a disciplined and obedient majority. But later on, after the liquidation of the subversive movement when the executive power attempted to maintain for an indefinite period of time the suspension of public liberties and basic rights, it was then that the difficulties with the Parliament commenced. The president encountered a growing objection, even among its own majority, until it reached the point in which Congress refused to vote any further measures that threatened the freedom of the individuals considered to be superfluous.

It is true, however, that the prestige of the Uruguayan politicians was already undermined and that there was a widespread public criticism. But let's put the record straight: the great shortcomings and affairs that hit the country in all cases emanated from those political sectors that supported the regime and subsequently identified themselves with the coup, or at least did not belong to those who opposed it. I am convinced that the people highly regarded the Parliament as the defender of public morality. There was a basic trust that it was an organ which controlled the behavior of the rulers. A clear sign of lack of prestige can be traced through popular indifference; but when the Senate or the House of Representatives discussed such matters, one could find from the early hours of the day queues of citizens trying to secure a place in public gallery. Hence, the common person did not fail to express his concern about the fate of the democratic institutions.

One has, however, to remember that the situation in Uruguay was different from events in other countries where a threatened government may have received the support of a large segment of its population. In Allende's Chile, people were ready to commit themselves entirely to fight against the regime, others were indifferent, but there was an enormous contingent ready to sacrifice anything in order to defend *their* government. In Uruguay, we had the case of a bad government that was getting worse; it was the government itself that subverted the institutional order. In Latin America, to defend Parliament is quite a distinct phenomenon, it is like defending an abstract idea; it is impossible to personalize or to identify it with those who exercise power. The popular reaction in Uruguay had, therefore, to revert back to the defense of some basic values, such as the institutional system and the democratic traditions of the country. And even so, the intensity of the reaction was impressive. The general strike rapidly bypassed even the directives of some trade unionists and became a tenacious struggle for liberty. Facing brutal repression, with its leaders and thousands of its members imprisoned, even when threatened with a loss of jobs, the workers resisted for fifteen days. On July 9, 1973, thousands of people, passing the word from mouth to mouth, converged into the main streets of Montevideo and with no arms in their hands, faced the onslaught of the army and police massacring them. What else could the people be expected to do, facing a regime with the highest ratio of political prisoners in the world, with all liberties suppressed, and when repression becomes more severe every day?

There is a clear answer. The Uruguay people have not surrendered. In spite of the reign of terror and fear, the military rulers have remained isolated. Thus, no framework of popular support for the regime has been organized; only a few individuals with an outstanding spiritual emptiness agree to fill the higher positions of government. In reality, people did what they could. And it was much. But with the passing of time, it became clear that one could not face the well-equipped army and police, ready to kill.

These and other comments cannot, obviously, be isolated from my personal and emotional involvement. A protagonist of such a dramatic process cannot claim to present a dispassionate view. It is, therefore, of help to read in this book a systematic analysis from someone who, although coming from the world of academics, was exposed to the misdeeds of the military regime in Uruguay. The involvement of the author with the problem of our concern is not exclusively based on a cool "pure science" approach; the Uruguayans will never forget that Dr. Kaufman was also the initiator, organizer and permanent inspirator of the world campaign that has denounced the systematic violation of human rights by the tyranny that rules my country.

Although I wish the publisher great success with the sale of this book, let me also hope that in a short time the contents may become obsolete and a final chapter will be needed: the revival of democracy in Uruguay. I claim as of now the honour of again writing the new foreword.

Senator Wilson Ferreira Aldunate

Preface

When I originally began doing research on Uruguay, I could in no way foresee how deeply attached I would eventually become to the fate of this small and once prestigious country.

Most of the data was compiled during two visits to Montevideo in October 1972 and April 1973, when I started to grasp that the growing involvement of the military had launched a perhaps uncontrollable movement which would radically change the institutional setting of Uruguay. The June 1973 *autogolpe*, resulting in the dissolution of Parliament, was the catalyst provoking my decision to embark upon a serious analysis of this dramatic change and the characteristics of the decision-making process. Shortly after the first draft of the manuscript of this book was prepared, I was invited to join the Amnesty International Secretariat in London during my sabbatical to do research on human rights in some Latin American countries and amongst them, Uruguay. What was previously an intellectual adventure, aroused by an academic spirit of inquiry, in no time became a confrontation with a vivid documentation of cases of torture, death under torture, massive imprisonment, and kidnappings. If already difficult at the early stages to effectively maintain complete neutrality towards the subject matter, I have admittedly since adopted a critical attitude toward the repressive character of the regime. Furthermore, my feelings of involvement were strengthened by a dramatic episode in May 1976, when from London, Amnesty International and I were personally unsuccessful in trying to save the lives of two Uruguayan parliamentarians kidnapped in Buenos Aires whose bodies were discovered massacred forty-eight hours later. A third sought personality, the major exponent of Uruguay's democratic opposition, Senator Wilson Ferreira Aldunate, narrowly escaped death with our help.

This painful specialization on the repressive situation in Uruguay was the reason for the invitation extended to me to testify in hearings on human rights in Uruguay. Congressman Donald Fraser invited me to speak in front of the Subcommittee of International Organizations of the Committee of Foreign Relations of the House of Representatives and submit testimony in July 1976, together with Professor Martin Weinstein. My task was to analyze whether there was a pattern of gross violations of human rights in Uruguay, and the abundant evidence in the Amnesty International archives unequivocally corroborated the existence of such a regrettable and consistent pattern. Two months later, both houses of Congress ratified the decision of suspending military aid to Uruguay based on legislation that conditioned such aid on minimal respect of human rights. The White House unexpectedly refrained from vetoing this resolution.

Back to the Hebrew University in Jerusalem, in the autumn of 1976, I was able to prepare the final draft of this book on Uruguay with a feeling of satisfaction—the justified ambition of many social scientists of producing research which is policy-relevant. Let us hope, then, that this work will provide a critical analysis of the role played by the internal and external forces in paving the way for the military takeover, and learning from their responsibility in the past, a rapid recovery of democracy in Uruguay will not fail to come in the very near future.

Acknowledgements

First, I wish to express my gratitude to those politicians, members of Parliament, diplomats, and friends in Uruguay who were so helpful in providing me with material and valuable comments, whom it would be better not to name, bearing in mind the present circumstances. A special mention is reserved for Nicholas ————, whose information proved to be so efficient and accurate. Special thanks are extended to Senator Wilson Ferreira Aldunate, from whom, in many long days of exile, I had the chance to more deeply grasp the intricacies of Uruguay's politics; to Professor Michael Brecher of the political science department of McGill University, for the thorough discussions that enabled me to explore the possibilities of using his decision-making framework in an unconventional way; and the late and beloved Professor Kalman Silvert, whose valuable comments on the manuscript were an important guideline for this work.

My appreciation goes to my friends and research students, Manuel Adler, Judith Shribman-Ron, and Moti Raz, for their help in compiling additional data in Jerusalem, and to the Central Research Fund and the Leonard Davis Institute for International Relations of the Hebrew University, whose generous grants made this research possible. Also, thanks goes to the Documentation Center of Amnesty International, which provided me with a most valuable opportunity to use their unique documentation on Uruguay.

Finally, I would like to dedicate this book to the memory of two talented and brave Uruguayan parliamentarians who paid with their lives for the privilege of raising their voices: Senator Zelmar Michelini and Congressman Héctor Gutiérrez Ruiz, whom I was honored to know and who enlightened my knowledge about their country in a short but fruitful correspondence, which was tragically interrupted by their assassination.

1.
Methodological Outline

Until the early 1970s, Uruguay held a worldwide reputation as a democratic island in Latin America. It maintained during the greater part of the twentieth century a collective executive system, thus acquiring the distinction of the "Switzerland of South America."[1] The constitutional tradition was emphasized by a nonpersonalist and nonauthoritarian executive, political stability, high standard of living, and high educational and cultural level.[2]

The military has shattered this established tradition. Over a period of two years, their growing involvement in politics ended with their absolute control over the executive. What has been popularly called the *autogolpe* (self-coup), placing President Bordaberry at the mercy of the army, was a slow process if compared with the rapid takeovers in other Latin American countries. The events of this coup can be divided into three stages: October 1972; February 1973; and June 1973.[3] Characteristic of each period was the open clash between the civil and military powers resulting in concessions by one or both of the two sides. The conflict expressed itself in reciprocal allegations between members of the legislative branch and the military elite; in the beginning, the president sided with Congress but gradually surrendered to military pressure, tipping the delicate balance of power in favor of the army. Congressmen, who in the earlier stages vigorously denounced the arbitrary attitude of the army, became the target of accusations from the military. They were forced to adopt a defensive stance, one that, however, failed to prevent its eventual dissolution. The peculiar rhythm and character of the military coup in Uruguay is undoubtedly related to its being the first for this country during the last century, and it is the aim of this study to analyze this fundamental transformation.

The book is devoted to an analysis of the major internal and external variables that have affected political developments in Uruguay; accordingly, the categories of the conceptual framework of foreign policy decision making,

1

Figure 1
Research Design

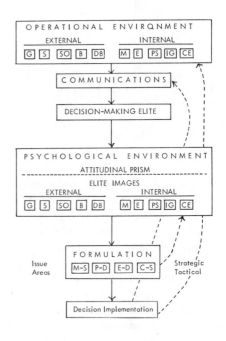

INPUTS

OPERATIONAL ENVIRONMENT

External:	Global	(G)
	Subordinate	(S)
	Subordinate Other	(SO)
	Bilateral	(B)
	Dominant Bilateral	(DB)

Internal:	Military Capability	(M)
	Economic Capability	(E)
	Political Structure	(PS)
	Interest Groups	(IG)
	Competing Elites	(CE)

COMMUNICATION—The transmission of data about the operational environment by mass media and face-to-face contacts

PSYCHOLOGICAL ENVIRONMENT

Attitudinal Prism: Ideology, historical legacy, personality predispositions

Elite Images: of the operational environment, including competing elites' advocacy and pressure potential

PROCESS

FORMULATION of strategic and tactical decisions in four issue areas:

Military-Security	(M-S)
Political-Diplomatic	(P-D)
Economic-Developm'l	(E-D)
Cultural-Status	(C-S)

IMPLEMENTATION of decisions by various structures: head of state, head of government, foreign office, etc.

OUTPUTS — the substance of acts or decisions

suggested by Brecher, Steinberg, and Stein, are adopted[4] (see Figure 1).

Although originally designed to analyze foreign policy decisions, its broad categories are applicable to political decision making in general, particularly in countries of penetrated systems where national politics are inextricably interwoven with external forces. As this is a pioneering case study for the application of this framework to the analysis of an "internal" policy decision, its comprehensiveness permits us to apply it to a decision such as launching a military coup.

Difficulties emerge, however, in attempting to clearly distinguish between internal and external political decisions in a region considered to be under the influence of one of the superpowers. Chile, on the one hand, is a clear-cut example of a case in which it is impossible to separate the domestic and external pressures that provoked the army's ousting of Allende. On the other hand, the successful invasion in 1954 of the military column in Guatemala, headed by

Colonel Castillo Armas, has traditionally been considered as an "external event" because it was initiated in foreign territory. The defeat of the constitutionalist pro-Bosch military sector in the Dominican Republic after the landing of U.S. troops in Santo Domingo in 1965 was also legitimately thought to be a product of an international crisis. Thus, to paraphrase Kissinger's "Domestic Structure and Foreign Policy,"[5] one cannot take the external environment as a given and declare that internal politics begin where foreign policy ends.

Although at first glance, changes in the political regime in Uruguay appear to have resulted from decisions taken by the military elite in conflict with other political forces, it is necessary to seek an explanation within a broader and more comprehensive framework. As to the relative influence of the various actors, although the elites and interest groups inside Uruguay seem to have greater weight than external forces, their indirect influence on the actors is, nevertheless, considerable. While some Latin American writers explain military intervention in politics as merely a culmination of United States policy,[6] most Latin Americanists reject such a proposition. Still others emphasize that military dictatorship is an inherent disease of the Latin American political culture.[7] We take the position that both internal and external factors are relevant to the problem of military intervention; in each case, then, it becomes necessary to define the period involved in the specific country and weigh the various possible variables.[8]

Several external influences upon the process of the military takeover in Uruguay are examined in the present analysis: the dominant role of the paramount superpower; the competitive influence of its two large neighbors, Argentina and Brazil; and the political developments in the Latin American region, which undoubtedly helped shape internal events in Uruguay. Internal determinants, focused upon after a brief consideration of the political structure and the economic situation of this country, are: the role of the traditional political parties, as expressed for the most part, in the Uruguayan Congress; the political and personality weakness of the president; the role of the electoral left, as shown through the mobilization of the trade unions and university groups; the repercussions of the urban guerrilla movement—the Tupamaros—and their incipient counterparts, the right-wing paramilitary organizations; the position of important pressure groups, such as the rural and upper-class circles, the church, and the mass media; and public opinion vis-à-vis the growing military involvement.

The interaction of these factors, as viewed by the author, are inserted into what Brecher calls the "operational environment." However, a study of how the constraints of these operating forces are perceived by the decision-making elite is equally crucial to our explanation. In this research, the major source of power driving the political process in Uruguay to a military takeover is unequivocably the army generals. It therefore becomes incumbent to grasp their basic beliefs and attitudes toward the political, social, and economic problems of the country. It is thus through their attitudinal prism that the internal and external constraints or stimulus are understood.

Furthermore, an attempt is made to determine the time at which the strategic decision of the army to assume absolute power was adopted. It is important to establish whether there was a distinct point in the process of military involvement that could explain such an extreme measure, or if the relevant moves should more appropriately be considered as a number of tactical decisions leading to an increasing trend of military responsibilities in the conduct of state affairs.

The major findings of this study are finally used to test various hypotheses related to military involvement as an independent variable, both in a general theoretical context and in the more particular cases of developing countries in Latin America.

Obviously, the application of this general research framework to a case study of a developing country under the sphere of influence of a single superpower presents several methodological problems, which are examined in the conclusion of this book. In a brief comparison with the Chilean experience, this last chapter also assesses the utility of introducing a multilevel approach (international system, regional, and domestic influences) to the decision-making process in abrupt changes of regimes.

NOTES

1. Nearly all writings on Uruguay start with such a reference. See, for instance, articles of Samuel Shapiro, "Uruguay's Lost Paradise," *Current History* 62 (1972):98–104; or Héctor Gutiérrez Ruiz, "Uruguay: Las Fuerzas Armadas y la realidad del pais," *Estrategia* 19–20 (1972, 1973):17–30.

2. Uruguay and Chile are, respectively, listed first and second as civilian countries in a table measuring the number of years of civilian (64) and military (5) presidents from 1901–1969, while the total Latin American average is 40.5 for civilian and 28.5 for military presidents. Basic data taken from Russel H. Fitzgibbon, "Components of Political Change in Latin America," *Journal of Inter-American Studies and World Affairs* 12 (1970):193. In general indices of political development ("A scale of political change relevant to democracy"), the general consensus of the specialists' responses was to rank Uruguay first out of twenty Latin American countries. See R.H. Fitzgibbon and Kenneth F. Johnson, "Measurement of Latin American Political Change," *American Political Science Review* 55 (1961):518.

3. For a detailed chronological description of major events preceding the crisis, see the Appendix. The events are divided into a series of stages whose cumulative effect brought about the final takeover.

4. For a comprehensive explanation of their approach, see M. Brecher, B. Steinberg, and J. Stein, "A Framework for Research on Foreign Policy Behavior," *The Journal of Conflict Resolution* (1969):75–101.

5. Henry Kissinger, "Domestic Structure and Foreign Policy," in *International Politics and Foreign Policy*, ed. James N. Rosenau (New York: Free Press, 1969), pp. 261–75.

6. Alonso Aguilar, *Pan-Americanism, from Monroe to the Present* (London: Modern Reader, 1968); Horacio L. Venerón, *Estados Unidos y las Fuerzas Armadas de América Latina* (Buenos Aires: Ed. Periferia, 1971), or Juan Bosch, *Pentagonism: A Substitute for Imperialism* (New York: Grove Press, 1968).

7. See, for instance, Wolf's evaluation: "Dictatorships, military or otherwise, are a frequent and disturbing phenomenon in Latin America. But their occurrence and recurrence are not properly attributable to simple causes like military aid or defense programs. Indeed, these factors do not appear to play a significant role in the process at all. Rather, the explanation lies in a complex set of influences rooted in Latin American history, social structure and political tradition." Charles Wolf, "The Political Effects of Military Programs: Some Indication from Latin America," *Orbis* 8 (1965):890.

8. For a successful analysis of the combination of both the internal and external environmental influences, see an article by John Duncan Powell, "Military Assistance and Militarism in Latin America," *Western Political Quarterly* 18 (1965):382–92.

2.
Operational Environment:
External Setting

The total international system is presently seen as consisting of military bipolarity and political multipolarity;[1] while the nuclear capabilities of the United States and the USSR encompass a dimension of supremacy vis-à-vis other powers, the reciprocal deterrence caused by the delicate "balance of terror" permits a more active involvement of countries such as France, China, or West Germany in international politics.

In general, the vacuum left by the retreating colonial powers has paved the way for a new policy of neocolonialism by these very countries, with the added presence of the superpowers: the United States, the Soviet Union, and China. Today this situation prevails in most of Afro-Asia, where secondary powers play a political role as great as that of the superpowers: France in some Francophone African countries; Great Britain in some of the Commonwealth countries; China in North Korea, and so on.

However, this is not the case in the two regions bordering upon the super-powers: Eastern Europe and Latin America, where the Soviet Union and the United States, respectively, maintain a position of quasi-absolute control. The possibilities of change in the internal or foreign policies of a Latin American country are generally much more restricted when compared with Afro-Asian states; even with less power, the latter enjoy greater independence precisely because of the political multipolarity and big power competition. In this case study, Washington has had the dominant influence; since World War II, Uruguay has generally supported United States policies and has been cautious toward extracontinental powers.

Sporadic references to the Soviet Union by Uruguayan decision-makers cannot be taken as an indication of successful Russian influence in Uruguay.

Their role in the process leading to the *autogolpe* is significant, even as an indirect source of support to the Communist-oriented electoral front. Moscow certainly disapproved of the violent option adopted by the Tupamaros and openly disassociated itself from such ventures. Altogether, it kept a very low profile, as a best guarantee for maintaining presence in Uruguay.

An example of the limitations affecting Soviet activity in this country is exemplified when a few months after the *autogolpe*, President Bordaberry presented the Soviet ambassador in Montevideo, Nikolai Demidov, with a note stating, in a "severe form" ... "to stop interfering in the international or internal policy of Uruguay because ... [of] the distribution of a Press bulletin containing a declaration of the Communist Party of the Soviet Union, condemning the military regime in ... Chile."[2]

In 1966, four Soviet diplomats were expelled from Montevideo because of a speech by a Soviet delegate at the Tri-Continental Conference in Havana, in which sympathy was expressed towards guerrilla movements in certain countries (Uruguay not among them). Moscow denied that the delegate in Cuba spoke in an official capacity, but rather as a representative of a "public institution" (the USSR Trade Unions).[3]

Accusations of a threat of "international Communism" to Uruguay do not necessarily reflect real Soviet activity but are more often a warning against left-wing activity in the country, or a preventive sign to Soviet diplomats that is sporadically expressed in order that the embassy maintains a low level of activity. Of even less significance has been the political impact in Uruguay of countries such as Communist China. With some trade links with Uruguay, Peking has been unwilling to undermine them, as they have found no clear alternative among the left which has been sympathetic towards their particular brand of communism. There was no permanent Chinese presence due to the lack of diplomatic relations, and altogether it seems as if China has given priority to the development of positive relations with the regimes of the larger countries of South America.

With the exception of its participation as an observer in the 1972 nonaligned conference of Georgetown, Guayana, Uruguay's involvement with the neutralist movement has been consistently kept at a minimum. The European ethnic composition of Uruguay's population, its Western cultural values, and the sense of geopolitical smallness has limited any desire for an active foreign policy in a nonaligned framework. Uruguay's diplomatic activity has been uniformly aimed at creating an image of a liberal supporter of the West, adhering to its basic principles while often resenting violations by any type of totalitarian deviations. Traditionally, Western Europe has been the major trading partner of Uruguay,[4] and in this context, one could expect that political strings would be attached to such a relationship. However, these allies of the United States have not felt compelled to compete for political influence in this country. The absence of a strong Christian Democratic movement and any type of Social Democratic party in Uruguay has reduced to an even greater extent the level of ideological interest of the European counterparts in the outcome of political events in Montevideo. It was only *post factum*, when allegations of serious violations of human rights by the military authorities were widely circulated, that the European Parliament condemned such atrocities and influenced the authorities of the European Common Market not to provide the Uruguayan regime with any terms of preferential trade.[5]

Even Cuba's direct influence has been secondary. Without diplomatic links, the Havana leaders expressed steady but decreasing verbal support for the Tupamaros urban guerrillas, but no sizable material help was extended. Although at the beginning of the Tupamaro's activity, Cuba's position was that of defending the concept of rural guerrillas, after Ché Guevara's defeat in Bolivia, declaratory backing was extended also to urban guerrillas. Later, with the advent of the Allende regime to power, greater sympathy was expressed by the Cuban propaganda machine with the "electoral" left in Uruguay. Consequently, the Cubans followed with declarations in favor of the Frente Amplio in the last elections, as well as to the FIDEL in the previous ones. However, the major impact of revolutionary Cuba was in strengthening the ideological background of the left and the inclination toward the use of armed struggle.[6]

DOMINANT BILATERAL: THE UNITED STATES

It is difficult to assess the extent of the United States' involvement in the process of militarization in Uruguay, as there was no direct and open intervention. The first question thus becomes whether American interests in Uruguay were sufficiently vital to provoke intervention. From an economic perspective, an American presence is not felt as strongly there as in other Latin American countries.[7] The total amount of investments is relatively low and unrelated to the main Uruguayan exports, meat and agriculture products, but is mainly concentrated in finance and banking.[8] In 1970, annual sales by affiliates of U.S. firms engaged in manufacturing were estimated at approximately $59 million.[9] In a sense, Uruguayan economic dependence upon the United States developed mostly through loans and an accumulated foreign debt related to sources of international credit, where Washington exercises considerable control.[10] At the bilateral level, the total economic assistance from the United States to Uruguay was relatively small; in the period from 1946 to the middle of 1975, it amounted to $123.6 million, including loans and grants from the U.S. Agency for International Development (AID).[11]

Perhaps of more consequence to American interests are military-strategic considerations. As a buffer state between the two "big" South American powers, Uruguay can serve as a separating element in case of conflict or as a base of influence when Argentina or Brazil fail to follow the general pro-American pattern. Furthermore, the strategic importance of the River Plate basin has been repeatedly stressed.[12] The river provides a communication system for five countries; the waters are a source for irrigation and for hydro-electric power; its platform is believed to contain considerable oil reserves. The high rate of economic development in Brazil, the construction of a road network towards Paraguay and Uruguay, and the building of hydroelectric plants on regional waterways have created certain tensions with Argentina. Uruguay's role as a loyal ally of the United States is a guarantee of free navigation at the River Plate mouth.

Political considerations have also played a noteworthy role. The threat of internal revolt resulting from urban guerrillas or the risk of the left's gaining power through democratic elections has made the United States sensitive to the potential loss of one of its more faithful and stabler friends. Furthermore, the cumulative effect on the subsystem of such a change was perceived as even more dangerous: while Peru and Chile had already emancipated themselves by that time from American tutelage, Argentinian politics were moving towards an expected Peronist victory.

Following the victory of the left in Chile, the potential loss of the second democratic regime of South America was considered to be a serious setback for the United States. At the same time, even inside Uruguayan ruling circles, an erosion of the pro-American line began to be felt. A slightly more independent foreign policy was conceived by the Uruguayan Foreign Minister Blanco. During a general debate about the future role of inter-American cooperation at the General Assembly of the OAS meeting in April 1973, he expressed a position partially in agreement with the criticism of U.S. activity in Latin America and suggested the creation of a separate representative Latin American regional organization, while still maintaining the existence of the Organization of American States.[13]

Finally, Uruguay has traditionally served as a distribution center of left-wing literature throughout the continent.[14] In order to counteract this threat, the United States created a cultural and propaganda campaign using the United States Information Service, the American Institute for Free Labor Development, and by supplying articles to the daily press and films to the private television stations.

Senator Erro, in exile and imprisoned in Argentina until 1976, denounced the United States as the main instigator of the *autogolpe* through the use of its embassy in Montevideo, the military mission in the Laguna Sauce base, and the CIA.[15] Denunciations of American involvement in internal affairs were voiced repeatedly in the Uruguayan Parliament while it was still functioning, not only in relation to the training of the police and military forces, but also in the organization of the paramilitary Escuadrón de la Muerte (Death Squad).[16]

U.S. involvement in the organization, training and equipping of Uruguay's Death Squad is abundantly described in the testimony of Nelson Bardesio, a police photographer and Death Squad member who was kidnapped and interrogated by *Tupamaro* guerrillas in 1972. In his testimony (which was recorded in the presence of the President of Uruguay's Chamber of Deputies), Bardesio affirmed that the Department of Information and Intelligence (DII)—a government agency that provided an official cover for the Death Squad—was set up with the advice and financial assistance of U.S. Public Safety Advisor William Cantrell. Bardesio also testified that Cantrell (whom he sometimes served as chauffeur) made daily trips between the DII, Montevideo police headquarters and the U.S. Embassy to insure steady transfer of intelligence data and effective coordination of extra-legal operations.[17]

A more general report about U.S. involvement was submitted to Senator W. Fulbright, at the time chairman of the Senate Committee for Foreign Relations, by William Higgs, executive director of the Committee for an Open Society, in which additional topics such as the introduction of modern identification procedures and telephone tappings[18] were raised.

While direct military intervention in distant South American countries has been generally ruled out by the United States, incidents in neighboring countries of Uruguay have confirmed the use of such covert methods. Therefore, it would, perhaps, be better to adopt a more general thesis, that American policy toward Uruguay stimulated the military takeover. By attaching growing importance to the military in the antisubversive campaigns, by legitimatizing and advising them in their initial steps into politics, and by courting them after each political success, the United States undoubtedly performed an important role as an indirect source of strength.

The public image of the Uruguayan armed forces improved through their successful repression of the Tupamaros. Antisubversive training was extended by the U.S. through the Office of Public Safety of the Agency for International Development, the programs of the International Police Academy, including the training of Uruguayans in the United States, the sending of police experts to Uruguay, and the supply of modern equipment for the improvement of patrol, riot control, police management, investigations, and communications.[19] Furthermore, before the Military Assistance Treaty between the United States and Uruguay expired (it needed to be renewed in 1970), during a two-year period, France continuously offered a supply of $100 million of armaments in easy and long-term payments.[20] In order to assure the successful renewal of the treaty, the U.S. applied pressure at a period when, because of the internal threat, the Uruguayan army was transforming itself from a decorative force to an effective and dynamic body, a last resort against insurgency.

Conceivably, U.S. inspired activities could have indirectly influenced the military. The "civic action" program launched through American initiative (construction of roads, hospitals, classrooms) could have both produced a better image of the army in the eyes of the public, as well as created a greater awareness within the military about their duties in the field of national development.

In addition, the nomination of a new American ambassador, Ernst Siracusa, is thought to have uniquely contributed to the military takeover. Two weeks prior to the dissolution of Congress in Uruguay, an Argentinian newspaper described his background as enriched by clandestine participation in coups in other Latin American countries such as Honduras, Guatemala, Peru and Bolivia. The article predicted that "Siracusa's mission appears at the time when governmental and diplomatic circles in Washington considered irreversible the developments in Uruguay toward a military government," and at the same time "to preserve the Brazilian rear-guard of the possibility that in Montevideo there will be established a nationalistic-populist regime." [21] Therefore it was perhaps not in initiating the process, but in accompanying, influencing, and attempting to divert it to a pro-American course that the Americans encouraged the military in Uruguay to compete for political power against the traditional elite. The rapid escalation that is sometimes produced by the dynamics of the process itself, is described by Bosch as an aspect of the "pentagonistic" method: "Once control of the armed forces was firmly taken, every attempt on the part of the governors of this country to govern independently was blocked with the threat of a military coup, and frequently the coup has come about by the simple exercise of excessive pentagonist power." [22]

SUBORDINATE SYSTEM:
THE LATIN AMERICAN SUBSYSTEM

In analyzing an event such as the incidence of dictatorship in Latin America, Needler concludes that factors producing such phenomena are in part cyclical. [23] In other words, we often find abrupt ups and downs in the political process in the continent; once occurring in one or a few Latin American countries, the curve rapidly rises to include most of the elements of the subsystem. In our case, we can discern a number of processes that strengthened the trend towards the military's political involvement in Uruguay. First, the expansion of guerrilla movements in Latin America in the 1960s and their defeat indirectly encouraged other processes, such as the creation of electoralist left-wing popular fronts and the process of a military takeover in several countries. Furthermore, the changing political orientation of Latin American regimes led to a polarization within the inter-American framework at the beginning of the 1970s, also influencing the Uruguayan process.

Guerrilla Warfare

The Tupamaros, originating in 1962, reached a peak of activity in 1968 following the defeat of the Ejercito de Liberación Nacional—ELN (Guevara's rural guerrilla expedition in Bolivia). Raising the fallen banner, they kept the flame alive on the continent until the early 1970s. During the decade of the sixties, all the countries in South America, excluding Ecuador, were affected by the existence of such guerrilla movements in one form or another. In Bolivia, Peru, Venezuela, and Columbia, they mainly took the form of rural movements, while in Paraguay, the attempt failed during its initial stage. In Brazil, Uruguay, Argentina, and to some extent, Chile, we witnessed the organization of an urban guerrilla network. While there can be no disagreement over the fact that the disruption of normal life in Uruguay and the threat to the ruling elite by the Tupamaros were determining factors in the changing role of the army, similar phenomena in other countries of the continent also affected and stimulated new processes influencing the events within.

Popular Fronts

On the other hand, there was the formation of popular fronts, Communist-inspired, but including socialists and radicals, splinter groups of traditional center parties and left-wing Catholic participants. Particularly after the victory in the 1970 elections in Chile, similar attempts were made in Argentina, with the formation of the Encuentro Nacional de los Argentinos (National Encounter of the Argentinians, ENA), later changed in the 1973 elections to the Alianza Popular Revolucionaria (Popular Revolutionary Alliance, APR). In Venezuela during preparations for the 1973 elections, the Communists tried to create a similar front with the "Nueva Fuerza" (New Force), including the Movimiento Electoral del Pueblo (Electoral Movement of the People, MEP) and other parties, but suffered a serious setback with the walkout of the important center party, Union Republicana Democratica (Republican Democratic Union, URD). Even under dictatorial regimes such as Bolivia's, there were beginnings of the organization of an opposition center-left front.

In a Uruguay that resembled the legalistic and parliamentarian tradition of Chile, events in the latter could not fail to carry their weight. While the idea of the Popular Front in Uruguay is traceable to the early 1960s, it was only from 1971 that the Wide Front constituted a real threat.

While the revolution by guerrilla warfare was almost completely extinguished by the early seventies, the electoral option was now presented as a growing threat to American hegemony. Kissinger perceived the dangers of the "domino theory" not only in the regional framework of Latin America, but he also feared that its expansion in this continent would have severe repercussions in the southern countries of Europe.[24] In this larger picture, the relative electoral success of the Wide Front had an aggravating effect, potentially greater than if it would have been an isolated event.

Militaristic Drive

Guerrilla warfare throughout Latin America stimulated a high level of military involvement in the internal problems of various countries in the region; the beginning through counterinsurgency actions and later by the assumption of greater responsibility in the running of their respective countries. While their policy orientation could now adopt different forms (developmental pro-American, nationalist-reformist-neutralistic or traditional), a rapid process of "militarization" of political power took place. If in 1954, out of the twenty governments in the subsystem, twelve were legacies of coups d'etat, the cycle was lowered by 1961 to only two (Paraguay and Haiti). From 1962, the trend took an about-face with coups in Argentina, Bolivia, Brazil, and the Dominican Republic, among others. By the early 1970s, in addition to the military or quasi-military regimes in Central America, with the exception of Costa Rica and Mexico, the army ruled in the south in Peru, Argentina, Brazil, Paraguay, Bolivia, and Ecuador. It strongly influenced the civil regimes of Colombia and Venezuela, and in Chile, the growing involvement of the military in political life was shown by repeated participation of the head of the three armed forces branches in Allende's successive Cabinets, only a few weeks after the *autogolpe* by the coup of Gral, Pinochet, and his junta. The influence of external events was demonstrated in December 1972, when President Bordaberry justified himself by claiming that it was necessary to increase involvement of the military in the country's affairs, as it was the case "elsewhere in the world."[25]

The importance of several political processes in the subsystem, as interlinked by chronologically separate situations, has been stressed; another view, however, argues that the nationalistic-reformist military regimes of Peru and the Popular Unity civilian front in Chile were a simultaneously introduced stimulus within Uruguay for the creation of a leftist nationalistic military-civilian coalition, a process that was diverted by the June 1973 *autogolpe*.[26]

Finally, it is necessary to examine the foreign-policy orientation of Latin American regimes towards the regional structure, and the United States' role in the inter-American subsystem at our particular time of study. It is still another input into the processes, creating a new situation which was surely reflected in Uruguay. After a continuous predominance within the Pan-American system, the United States found at the beginning of 1973, for the first time, great difficulties in remaining the bloc leader. Until then, the State Department had always managed to achieve a semiautomatic two-thirds of the votes for passing important motions at the Organization of American States. By 1973, it nearly failed to mobilize the one-third required to stop motions antagonistic to the United States interests. We faced a polarization of forces on what came to be known as the "Brasilia-Washington Axis" on the one hand, and the "Havana-Lima Axis" on the other. The former, representing the traditional pro-American line, included Brazil and the more economically backward and dictorial small Caribbean, Central American, and South American states. The second challenged U.S. hegemony and was strengthened by the addition of the nationalistic military regimes in Panama and Ecuador, and by the Popular Unity Victory in Chile. Faced with having to make a choice, more and more Latin American countries supported the critical arguments of the Havana-Lima Axis, against the United States. Mexico, Argentina, Venezuela, Colombia, and Costa Rica favored at least one of the following arguments: restructuring of the inter-American system, condemnation of American multinational corporations involved in the politics of Latin American countries, acceptance of the 200-mile territorial sea limit, support for Panama's demand for sovereignty over the Canal Zone and for Cuba's reintegration into the OAS, criticism of America's selling of Latin American strategic mineral reserves on the world market and the raising of import custom duties by Washington. By early 1973, in an ECLA meeting (UN Economic Commission for Latin America) in Ecuador, an OAS meeting in Washingon, and a UN Security Council meeting in Panama City, the United States faced growing opposition. Events in Uruguay could conceivably have affected the already disfavorable balance, and the United States thus tried influencing Uruguayan foreign policy, which was timidly approaching the "middle way" already adopted by Argentina and Venezuela. The *autogolpe* guaranteed Uruguay's return to the traditional pro-American camp, highly significant in light of its spreading effect on other countries in the subsystem.

Thus, in a period of less than two years, the whole picture in the Southern Cone changed radically, and by 1975 showed a rather homogeneous concentration of military regimes. Uruguay's immediate neighbors played a salient role in its political developments. Paraguay's ambassador in Montevideo was accused of collaboration with the Death Squad, maintaining contacts with the army, and financing right-wing publications;[27] the inputs of Argentina and Brazil were of a larger magnitude and deserve to be treated separately.

OTHER BILATERAL:
ARGENTINA AND BRAZIL

Uruguay's geopolitical position as a buffer state between the giants of South America, Argentina and Brazil, is a well-known feature. The need for Uruguay to keep a delicate balance in its policy towards the two as a means of assuring independence has been consistently maintained from the first days of the creation of the Oriental Uruguay Republic. By siding more with the passive neighbor, the temporary ambitions of the more agressive one were limited and restricted.

By the beginning of the period of our interest, we find in both Argentina and Brazil military dictatorships of a right-wing character. Facing the problems of terrorism in their territories, the relative success or failure of the guerrilla movement in Uruguay had direct repercussions on their own internal security. At this time, an old dispute over hegemony in the South American countries erupted, mainly due to the jealousy of the Argentinian ruling junta toward Brazil's rapid development and economic expansion into the smaller neighboring countries. While Brazil executed a more energetic and steadfast policy for gaining influence in Uruguay, Argentina adopted a more defensive stance, being weakened by the discontinuity with the change of regimes in 1973.

Argentina's involvement with the Uruguayan Army was felt in 1965 when the commander of the Argentinian Armed Forces, General Juan Carlos Onganía, sent a number of letters to his Uruguayan counterpart. One letter written to the general inspector of the army was submitted to the government by the latter, a letter prosposing a greater involvement of the army in politics, "in defense of our Christian and Western way of life and against the threats of red totalitarianism."[28] After becoming president, Onganía met twice in 1970 with Uruguayan President Pacheco Areco, who was energetically seeking ways to combat the growing waves of terrorism which were shaking his country. It is reported that in the meeting of "Club Remeros," they considered the feasibility of Argentinian military support in case of a breakdown of control resulting from the insurrectional threat in Uruguay.[29]

The Peronist regime of Cámpora's supported a policy of noninterference in Uruguayan affairs. However, other trends of Peronist foreign policy (reestablishment of relations with Cuba, close ties with the left-wing regime in Chile, Perón's praising comments about Ché Guevara, etc.) might have sharpened the United States' perception of the danger of a left-wing regime on both banks of the River Plate. The *autogolpe* took place a month before Perón replaced Cámpora, and most probably the timing was by no means entirely coincidental.

At a more general level, a crisis atmosphere developed, somewhat similar to the attitude of democratic Uruguay against the first dictatorial Peronist regime, but a mirror image this time in that a democratically elected regime in Argentina was now witnessing the military takeover in Uruguay. Buenos Aires became the major center of political refugees from Uruguay, and the press there was openly hostile to the new regime. However, the Argentinian government tried to reduce all sources of friction with Uruguay. Meetings between Perón and Bordaberry led to the signing of the "Treaty of Boundaries in the River Plate and its Marine Front," in November 1973,[30] bringing about a successful compromise to the long-term jurisdictional dispute over territorial waters.

The relationship with Brazil, beginning in the mid-sixties, clearly showed

Brazil's concern about the political instability in Uruguay. This is openly expressed in the government-controlled press by warning that *"Itamaraty* [Brazil's Foreign Ministry] cannot disregard the events that are taking place in Montevideo, not only because of the friendship that Brazil feels for the Uruguayan people, but because of the implications they may have on Brazilian security that could be compromised by such events."[31] "It is therefore considered that in case of an internal crisis and the eruption of a left-wing government . . .," it will be necessary for an intervention of the OAS type, such as carried out in Santo Domingo, preceded by the necessary consultations and made by the neighboring countries, Argentina and Brazil.[32]

Relations had already become tense after the Goulart regime was overthrown in 1964, with the Uruguayans accepting many of the persecuted Brazilian political leaders. Furthermore, the existence of large-scale smuggling of contraband livestock into Brazil was another source of friction. There were also later divergences over the question of the methods used against terrorism. While Uruguay adopted the hard line of not surrendering to guerrilla ultimatums for ransom and exchange of prisoners, Brazil, in spite of its "strongman" image, was following a pattern of concession to local guerrilla blackmail. This controversy sharpened over the kidnapping of the Brazilian consul in Montevideo, Dias Gomide, in which Uruguay maintained her intransigent line.

A steady increase of Brazilian economic influence within Uruguay[33] also occurred: investments in real estate; financing of loans to peasants while controlling the type of farming in the border provinces such as Rocha, Treinta y Tres Orientales; with an increase in Brazilian tourism to the most exclusive sea resorts; and the fruition of important joint development projects, such as Sete Quedas (Guaira Falls hydroelectric plant) and the bridge between Quarai and Artigas. In many ways, Uruguay came to be considered as a "petrol station" on the way from Brazil to Argentina. New roads and bridges financed by Montevideo helped to increase Brazilian tourism to Argentina.

Further Brazilian involvement was seen in its continuous vigilance over Uruguay's political developments. In 1967, a left-wing weekly in Uruguay[34] published a secret report quoting a memorandum drafted by the Military Staff of the High War School in Brazil, stressing the strategic importance of the neighboring countries and concern at the situation of "international Communism" in Uruguay and Cuba, citing the possible need for the use of Brazilian military force. After the death of Uruguayan President Gestido in 1969, his successor grew even more attached to Brazil.

In interpreting this growing rapprochement, one needs an explanation other than the traditional pro-Brazilian tendency of the "Colorado" leaders vis-à-vis the pro-Argentinian one of the "Blancos."[35] The "Uruguayan"[36] plan was an effort launched by Brazil through Home Affairs Minister Albuquerque Lima, with Bolivian President Alfredo Ovando acting as an envoy, persuading Pacheco Areco to adopt a hard line against left-wing organizations in general, thus beginning counterguerrilla activities. Further evidence of this trend is given by the Pacheco Areco meetings with the president of Brazil, Garrastazu Medici in May 1970, in which total agreement was widely publicized. By the 1971 elections in Uruguay, strong rumors were spread that Brazil had decided that in case of a left-wing victory, there was no alternative but military intervention, directly or through the Uruguayan military.

While the press in Buenos Aires was critical of the *autogolpe*, Brazil seemed to openly celebrate its development. The rapprochement of the military in Uruguay with the Brazilians seems quite outstanding. In Brazil, voices spoke of the convenience of having the Uruguayan connection[37] and announced that "Uruguay has entered the 'Brazilian Scheme.'"[38] These declarations provoked a Uruguayan reaction by civilian Foreign Minister Juan C. Blanco, who replied, "it was monstrous to think that Uruguay might cease to be independent." Still, the major trend in the military and also of President Bordaberry was that of accepting Brazil not only as a protective Big Brother, but also a pattern of development to be imitated, as well as a source for foreign investments.[39]

NOTES

1. Henry A. Kissinger, "The End of Bipolarity," in *The Theory and Practice of International Relations*, ed. F. Sonderman, William C. Olson, and David S. McClellan (Englewood Cliffs, N.J.: Prentice-Hall, 1970), pp. 50–54.

2. *La Opinión* (daily), Buenos Aires, September 29, 1973.

3. A clearcut example of exaggerated allegations can be found in the explanations given by the Uruguayan military after the vote against the proposals for a structural change suggested by Argentina's and Peru's delegations at the Conference of All-American Armies took place in Caracas in September 1973. Avoiding the major issues, Uruguayan delegate General Hugo Chaippe Posse diverted the issue by pointing out the threat of "international Communism" for Latin American countries in their development planning. *Clarín* (daily), Buenos Aires, September 13, 1973.

4. The major countries importing Uruguayan goods in the year 1973 were in order of importance: Federal Republic of Germany, Spain, Italy, the Netherlands, France, United Kingdom, Brazil, Belgium, Poland, Japan, and the U.S. These figures, taken from the Bank of London and *South American Review*, were quoted in *Amnesty International Document* (Uruguay campaign, Foreign Trade Briefing, International Secretariat, London, December 1975).

5. Reference to the text of telegram sent to President Bordaberry by the participants of the Second Interparliamentary Conference of the European Community with Latin America (Luxembourg, November 19–21, 1975).

6. Even so, the reference of the Tupamaros toward the means and aims used by the guerrilla in Cuba is vague, supportive only in principle. See "30 Preguntas a un Tupamaros," *Rojo Vivo* 180 (Montevideo, 1969); and Carlos A. Alverez and Jaime E. Canas, *Tupamaros, Fracaso del Che?* (Buenos Aires: Ediciones Orbe, 1969).

7. "In the domain of trade exchanges the predominance of commerce with the United States is

by no means a determining factor and does not create decisive links of dependence,'' Instituto de Estudios Políticos para América Latina (IEPAL), *Uruguay, Un País Sin Problemas en Crisis*, 2nd ed. (Montevideo: Estudios de Actualidad, 1965), p. 85.

8. According to Labrousse, the Chase Manhattan and its associates control nearly half of the capital banks in Uruguay. Alain Labrousse, *Les Tupamaros* (Paris: Combats, Seuil, 1971), p. 130.

9. Thomas E. Weil et al., *Area Handbook for Uruguay* (Washington: American University, 1971), p. 361.

10. Loans of the International Monetary Fund, the Bank of Inter-American Development, and the Bank of Reconstruction and Development are conditioned upon the adoption of previously agreed economic policies within the recipient country.

11. Weil, *Area Handbook*, p. 362.

12. Adalberto P. Lucchini, *Geopolítica del Cono Sur: La Cuenca del Plata* (Buenos Aires: Juárez Ed., 1976); and Bernardo Quagliotti de Bellis, *Uruguay en el Cono Sur—Destino Geopolítico* (Buenos Aires: Tierra Nueva, Colección Proceso 5/6, 1976).

13. *La Opinión* (daily), Buenos Aires, April 10, 1973; and *La Manāna* (daily), Montevideo, June 29, 1973.

14. For an official American description of Soviet propaganda activities, see, Weil, pp. 257-58.

15. *NACLA Newsletter* (1971).

16. The intervention of Senators Erro and Terra on the 7th and 8th, June 1972 session in the Senate, *Diario de Sesiones*, Cámara de Senadores, No. 18, pp. C.S. 532 and C.S. 519, respectively.

17. *LADOC*, Division for Latin America, United States Council of Churches, No. 49, June 1974, p. 24. The report follows the NACLA January 1974 article of Michael Klare and Nancy Stein. The text quotes Nardesio as speculating about the links between the AID and CIA, based on the experience in the Dominican Republic where the CIA used public safety programs as a cover.

18. Quoted in ''Uruguay y Ahora Qué?'' *Cuadernos de Crisis* 4 (1974): 10-11.

19. Ibid., p. 30. For a personal account about CIA in Uruguay during an earlier period, see Philip Agee, *CIA Diary* (Harmondsworth, England: Penguin, 1975).

20. Gabriel Ramírez, *Las Fuerzas Armadas Uruguayas en la Crisis Continental*, (Montevideo: Tierra Nueva, 1971). A report about the French operations was circulated among Congressmen by Senator Vasconcellos, pp. 124-25.

21. *La Opinión*, June 16, 1973.

22. Juan Bosch, *Pentagonism: A Substitute for Imperialism* (New York: Grove Press), p. 55.

23. Martin Needler, *Political Development in Latin America: Instability, Violence and Evolutionary Change* (New York: Random House, 1968), pp. 41-42.

24. Richard R. Fagen, ''The United States and Chile: Roots and Branches,''*Foreign Affairs*, 53 (1975):297-313.

25. *Kessing's Contemporary Archives* (1973), p. 25, 691.

26. *Cuestionario* 3 (1973):6.

27. Senator Erro's and Terra's intervention,*Diario de Sesiones*, Cámara de Senadores, (1972), C.S. 532, C.S. 543, respectively.

28. Gabriel Ramírez, p. 157.

29. Ibid., p. 170; Labrousse, *Les Tupamaros*, p. 152. See also Paulo R. Schilling, *El Nacionalismo Revolucionario* (Montevideo: Ed. Diálogo S.R.F., 1966).

30. See full text in *El Día* (daily), Montevideo, November 20, 1973.

31. Instituto de Estudios Políticos para América Latina, p. 126. Article published in *O Globo*.

32. See article of Felipe de Santamaría, ''La lenta y pacífica penetración brasileña en el Uruguay,''*La Opinión*, March 9, 1974. (Santamaría was the pen name for the late Senator Zelmar Michelini.)

33. C. Núñez, *Marcha* 1355 (1967).

34. *La Opinión*, June 29, 1973.

35. Weil, p. 299. Realistically speaking, such an observation must be made with caution. Historically, the Colorado party was put into power by a Brazilian invasion that deposed Berro's Blanco regime. However, the Argentinian government also intervened in order to aid General Flores and the Colorado party. One could better distinguish between the two parties by saying that, over time, the Blancos held a more isolationist and nationalist line, while the Colorados were more vulnerable to foreign influences, in particular to European trends.

36. Declarations of Brazilian geopolitician Enrique de Rocha in a speech to the Brazilian Chamber of Deputies, *Facts-on-File* (1973), p. 754.

37. *La Opinión*, June 29, 1973.

38. *Facts-on-File* (1973), p. 754. Still, Blanco would generally define Brazilian-Uruguayan relations as "without even a single point of friction." *La Opinión*, July 3, 1973.

39. Quoted from *La Nación* (Buenos Aires) in *Cuadernos de Crisis, Uruguay: Y Ahora Qué?* 4 (1974):11. The Brazilian influence can also be noted in the attempt of the Uruguayan generals to emulate, in the long run, the model adopted by the military in the former, by which two government-controlled parties would coexist under their strict control, with a president imposed or appointed with the consent of the armed forces.

3.
Operational Environment:
Internal Setting

When distinguishing the decision-making elite from other forces operating in the internal structure of a specific country, the reference is usually to the inner cabinet. The major criteria in deciding who belongs to the decision-making elite is the quantity of output originating from the actor in the political decision process, or more explicitly, the ability to influence strongly other persons by his political acts, rather than be influenced. In our case, it is quite clear that the central decision-making unit is found among the military leadership. What is normally one of several important interest groups came to play the major role in the adoption of political decisions, for by the time of the *autogolpe*, the president, traditional and left-wing parties, and all other associational and interest groups were reduced to the mercy of the generals' decisions. Therefore, we treat the military elite as the central decision-making unit and treat other forces as constraints of the internal setting to the freedom of choice, as perceived by the army generals.

POLITICAL STRUCTURE

Until 1968, Uruguay had a political system whose major feature was the search for consensus and "participationism." Attempts were made to allocate benefits to a wide spectrum of social and economic groups, and by the time its economic crisis became aggravated, the institutionalized techniques could no longer survive.[1]

During a large part of the twentieth century (1919–33, 1952–67), the government was formed through a Colegiado system, by which there was a National Council consisting of nine members from the majority and minority

21

Table 2
Electoral Results in Uruguay
(in thousands)

	1938	1942	1946	1950	1954	1958	1962*
Partido Colorado	219	328.5	310	433	444.1	378.4	521
P. Nacional (Blanco)	122	198.3	276	322	342.1	499	545
Unión Cívica (Christian)	14	24.4	35	36	44.2	36.5	35.7
P. Socialista	13	9	15.7	17	28.7	35	27
P. Comunista	5	14.3	32.6	19	19.5	26.7	40.8
U.D.R.	–	–	–	–	–	19.5	–

traditional parties, with the position of president (a nominal and ceremonial appointment) rotating every year amongst the members of the majority party. The distribution of administrative jobs was also according to a party key system, and while during most of the century the Colorado (Red) Party had a majority, the Blancos (White) were assured of representation. Stability was thus maintained, as is seen in Table 2, which shows a recurrent voting pattern.

In March 1959, after ninety-four years of failing to capture a majority, the Blancos gained power, thereby creating insecurity among large numbers of people occupying various offices on the Colorado ticket. Most of the high-ranking Army officers were also Colorados, and they now saw an uncertain future after retiring from a military career.[2]

In 1966, faced with a difficult economic situation and with incipient internal unrest, the voters agreed to return to the presidential system, in which the president, according to the 1967 Constitution, was granted broad powers. It was this trend towards authoritarianism that created some of the necessary preconditions for the transition from civilian to military rule.[3]

Another important aspect of the political structure is that the electoral system (lema) permits faction lists to nominate several presidential candidates, with the right to combine the votes for their candidate in favor of the candidate who has received the most votes.[4] In other words, the Blancos and Colorados may hold elections with each party nominating more than one candidate representing different factions; the elected president will be from the faction which received the largest number of votes from the party that polled the majority of votes. Therefore, as in this case, the president may have received a smaller number of votes than a candidate from the rival party, but be elected by the virtue of the total number of votes accumulated by his party. In American electoral terms, this phenomenon can be represented by the two parties holding their primaries on the same day as the national elections, thus consolidating the two stages in one act.

Finally, presidents have often been popular *caudillos* with a charismatic appeal, able to consolidate the leadership over their own party. For instance, Uruguay's national hero, José Gervasio Artigas, is a personalist legendary figure, and the prominent leader of the Colorado party of the late nineteenth and early twentieth centuries, José Batlle y Ordoñez, is still venerated by many as the "Father of Modern Uruguay." His relatives have since continued to maintain the myth of the "Batlle Clan" until today.

Furthermore, facing its first experience of a tripartisan system—with the created Broad Front of the left—two more features clearly point to the weakening of the political structure: (1) the Colorado party won the elections, but if the opposition votes are counted together, it suffered the greatest electoral defeat in its entire history; (2) internal divisions in the Colorado party did not present any clear consensus, as compared with the Blanco party where only one candidate was considered to have aspirations for the presidency. Therefore, Bordaberry received the lowest percentage of votes obtained by a winning candidate, and in fact, he was actually defeated by the Blanco leader Wilson Ferreira Aldunate, who was by far the most charismatic and popular leader in the 1971 elections. Hence, one could have opened this chapter by stating that the political structure of Uruguay hampered the placement of a solid civilian obstacle to the military drive. With the changes of the last decade, many of the traditional civilian structures were disrupted, and an added fragility emerged from the change of ruling parties as well as from the unsuitable personality characteristics of the new president.

THE ECONOMIC SITUATION

Undoubtedly, the serious economic crisis that befell Uruguay has had tremendous repercussions on its political developments. Not only has it weakened the existing socioeconomic structures and helped create a growing popular despair, but it has also shown the military that only an energetic, aggressive, and nonpartisan administration could save the country from total bankruptcy. Not only in its own eyes, but also in the opinion of large sectors of the population, could the army fulfill such a task.

The Uruguayan economy deteriorated steadily from the mid-fifties.[5] This crisis continued during the period of our study and can be seen through several indicators: the inflation rate and the rise in the cost of living rose at an astronomical rate. Inflation in the year 1967–68 reached 136%; 104% was estimated for the year ending in July 1973;[6] for the calendar year 1973, 100%.[7]

Table 3
Economic Indicators

Foreign Debt		Value of Exports		GNP per Capita	
Year	millions of US $	Year	millions of US $	Year	millions of US $
1969	35.0	1950	254	1955	712
1970	64.7	1955	183	1960	660
1971	108.5	1960	129	1965	640
1972	280.0	1965	191	1970	662
	(estimate)	1970	232	1971	635
		1971	205		

Source: Leandro Martín (Inter Press Service)   "La Opinión"
          December 20, 1972

The real wage continually declined. According to a report by the Uruguayan Institute of Economy, "the average of the private sector salaries in Montevideo for 1972 is 24% lower than the maximal salary for 1962 and 19.2% lower than the average for the years 1950-1967. In the public sector, salaries are 21.6% lower than the maximum for 1967, and 18.4% lower than the average for the years 1961-67. In relation to 1971, the salaries are lower than 1972 by 18%." [8]

In spite of the vigorous increases in price for primary goods on the world market (83% of Uruguayan exports consist of livestock and agricultural products), the balance of payments continued to be negative. Imports equalled exports in the best case, but the foreign debt was too great for a country passing through such a long period of economic crisis. It was estimated that Uruguay had to pay in the first quarter of 1973 (to foreign banks) the sum of $280 million, while the total exports for the year 1972 did not exceed $190 million. Livestock exports averaged 118,914 tons for the period 1921-30, while in the years 1967-71, it declined to 92,500 tons, increasing in 1972 to 104,000 tons. [9] In addition, the "meat-mountain" surplus of the European Community did not facilitate the increase of exports to these traditional markets.

Another indicator of the seriousness of Uruguay's economic crisis was the rate of devaluation. While in the early 1950s the Uruguayan peso was considered a hard and stable currency (an exchange rate of 3.46 to the dollar), by 1973, stemming from fantastic rates of devaluation sometimes as high as 200%, the peso was valued at 1,100 to the dollar. Table 3 presents some highly significant statistics about the deterioration of the economic situation.

Facing such a catastrophic deterioration, a large number of inhabitants began to emigrate, mostly to Argentina, and those with more definite plans to more remote countries. The fourth general census of the population, undertaken in 1963, gave the figure of 2,556,020 inhabitants for Uruguay. [10] On this basis, the

Table 4
Figures of Pensioners and Employees in Public
Administration

	1938	1955	1969
Public administration (sector employed)	57,500	166,400	213,000
Passive groups (pensioners)	no data	196,700	346,000

projections for the year 1975 varied between 3,040,000[11] and 3,377,000.[12] However, the census of May 21, 1975 showed an increase of scarcely 170,000, totalling after 12 years only 2,763,964.[13] The emigration figures for the last few years are estimated at 700,000. This number is a serious blow for the country's development, since most of the emigrants represented a valuable manpower element of the younger and more professional strata. Furthermore, the exodus produced a feeling of demoralization. The military's involvement was facilitated by this process, not only because it emphasized the need of a solution to this problem affecting the productivity of the country, but political opposition elements increasingly participated in the massive departures, fleeing the escalating repression.

At the same time, extensive social legislation created an advanced welfare structure that, even in normal times, was thought to be untenable. The economic crisis emphasized in a more acute way the maladjustment of these institutions to reality.

A large sector of the population relied on goverment salaries or allocations. With a population of slightly less than three million, the picture in 1970 was as follows in Table 4.[14]

An inefficient policy of distribution combined with panicky buying and the hoarding of basic products due to the price increases resulted in serious problems of supply and stock shortages. Oil, butter, and cigarettes were sporadically unavailable. Furthermore, the ban on domestic consumption of beef in order to increase exports during most of the period under focus explains the bitter resentment of the public and their fear for the future, in a country which had always been a traditional supplier of primary goods.

Another element leading to demoralization in the economic field was the growing reports of illegal economic activities of financial enterprises and individuals connected with governing circles, at both the executive and parliamentarian levels. Tax evasion, smuggling, false bookkeeping, profiteering from devaluation, corruption in the granting of public contracts to foreign enterprises, excessive expenses of high officials and legislators, and so on, added to the general feeling that the economic crisis, bad enough from objective conditions, was further compounded by mismanagement and corruption which would accelerate the country's ruin.

In this context, the March 1973 decision of Moisés Cohen, the minister of economy, to sell part of the gold reserves of the Central Bank worth $68 million, although rationally sound in light of Uruguay's heavy foreign currency debt, caused great apprehension and fear. The parliamentary opposition exploited such a decision so as to disseminate further criticism of the government. One of the major objections was related to the fact that the announcement about selling the gold reserves was made nearly a year later.

It was in conjunction with this economic situation that the appearance of the armed forces as a moralizing factor was considered by many citizens as perhaps the only way left for overcoming internal strife and applying *new* national criteria for rebuilding Uruguay's harassed economy. The military themselves paid attention to this image and spoke about the need for eradicating the diseases of corruption and disorganization, and for economic planning and development. A few months later, the *autogolpe* achievements, such as lifting the ban on the internal consumption of beef, and the announcement that all foreign debts ($100 million) for the year 1973 had been met[15] produced the anticipated effect of appeasing a population disturbed by the installation of a pseudo-dictatorship.

An important additional incentive for intervention was that in contrast with the bleak economic picture of the past, the military envisioned a bright future. This was based on the steep increase in price during the *autogolpe* of the two main exporting goods of Uruguay—wool and meat—whose value multiplied three- and four-fold. But unlike the stability of petro dollars, a ''takeoff'' based on Uruguay's basic goods could not be counted upon with certainty, as was later proven by the continuing economic crisis.

COMPETING ELITES

The military's struggle for power confronted at different times and with varying degrees of intensity both the president and the Congress. The first stage (October) was aimed at gaining control over the executive and then proceeding, with the support of the president, to confront the National Assembly. While the president surrendered to the army's claims, the partial concessions of the parliamentarians to the army were inadequate to assure full control of the military, thereby ending the crisis with the dissolution of both the House of Deputies and that of the Senate. Hereafter we shall refer, for the most part, to the confrontation between the army and the political elite of the traditional parties, the Blancos and Colorados. The left-wing Frente Amplio will be dealt with in the chapter dealing with the trade unions and university students, institutions from which it derived its political force. Frente Amplio acted less vigorously as an opposition force to military rule in Parliament than as the leading force of such important pressure groups.

The Legislative

Almost all Uruguayans consider themselves either Colorados or Blancos by birth, but in the 1972 Congress, we find a wide variety of tones, from the extreme nationalistic right to some splinter Colorado and Blanco left-wing groups that gave their votes to the presidential candidate of the Frente Amplio.[16] As the fragmentation of these traditional parties was undisputedly a symptom of the erosion of the established political system, it becomes confusing to follow the accepted categorization of the competing elites and classify them according to political parties. In this case study, one witnesses Parliament's acting very much as the "establishment," with a common fundamental interest: the prevalence and maintenance of the legal institutions. Above factional disputes, the threat to the Parliament's existence and the army's attack on individual members of the House was finally perceived not as a threat to some partisan groups, but to the system as a whole.

Under these conditions, President Bordaberry had great difficulties in obtaining a safe majority in Parliament.[17] By the "Acuerdo Nacional" (National Agreement), he was to receive the support of two Colorado and two Blanco groups, both gaining representation in the cabinet with ministers appointed by those factions. In both cases, the right-wings of the traditional parties were represented. The polarization inside the party was particularly felt among the Blancos, rivals to Bordaberry in the election, who were divided as to the strategy toward his government. While the majority faction, Por la Patria (For the Motherland) under Ferreira Aldunate's leadership was clearly for a civilian government, it was a minority group in some declarations. It advocated support for a stronger intervention: "That for the morale of our motherland, for its heroic tradition and for its predecessors, we totally and integrally accompany the Armed Forces and the authentically nationalist politicians."[18] It was a precarious situation, for without Blanco support, Bordaberry could only count on fifty-five legislators, while the opposition (Blanco and Frente Amplio) together had seventy-five representatives. It is precisely this delicate position that was exploited by the army, provoking a clash between the president and members of his own party in the coalition, thereby making him more dependent on the military.

The basic strategy of undermining and dividing the executive-legislative relations was accompanied by an effort to split the political forces in Parliament between the traditional parties and the left-wing opposition. It was achieved through collective accusations against legislators, aimed at reducing the prestige of the Congress in public opinion by exposing the corruption among its members, citing examples of special laws for the allocation of long-term mortgages for legislative members and staff, as well as a reduction of tax franchises, and the exposure of debts to the State Bank by presidential candidates.[19]

These allegations were echoed by the right-wing press that attacked the "Parliamentarian Syndicate" that blocked any attempt to fight corruption under the guise of safeguarding political institutions or protecting legality.[20] Another strategy aimed at undermining the traditional parties and gaining sympathy for the Frente Amplio was to condemn the pseudo-liberal attitude of "certain political sectors that try to obstruct the process of development installed during the institutional February crisis."[21] Furthermore, the exposure of corruption was only among parliamentarians of the traditional parties. Simultaneously, the army initially managed to ensure indifference by the representatives of the traditional parties towards the campaign launched against the left by accusing their Congressmen of cooperating, negotiating, or protecting the Tupamaros in order to secure themselves in the case of a victory by the subversive forces.

In its campaign against individual members, the military demanded the repeal of parliamentarian immunity in order to submit several congressmen to military courts. Interestingly, it began in October 1972 with Jorge Batlle Ibáñez, the presidential candidate of the rival Colorado list 15 who was a leading member of one of the groups comprising Bordaberry's coalition. Ibáñez was accused of corruption and imprisoned during the first crisis period.[22] This campaign was to be followed by one against another progovernmental Colorado, Amilcar Vasconcellos, who was accused of attempting to undermine the morale of the military by defaming them. This episode led to the second crisis. While in the first juncture, opposition leader Ferreira Aldunate identified himself in October with the civilian rule against the military's demands.[23] The situation differed after Bordaberry's submission to the army's ultimatum. On the Februrary 7, Ferreira met Generals Ventura Rodríguez and Cesar Martínez, both of whom initiated such a meeting in what they called the army's interest to maintain contacts with the leaders of the political factions, due to the dramatic events facing the nation.[24] On this occasion, the senator suggested that general elections be held within a period of a year, and in the meantime, a national cabinet coalition be formed, a widely-based cabinet "with a great Minister of Interior and a great Minister of National Defense."[25] It is not clear whether Bordaberry's resignation was requested, although it clearly encouraged the premature end of his mandate. However, what is more important is that it endorsed the principle of military involvement within the government machinery. As expressed by the Blanco chairman of the House of Representatives, and

Ferreira's loyal friend, Héctor Gutiérrez Ruiz: "The formula departed from a realistic view and did not determine the return of the Army to the barracks."[26] These talks were later used by the army itself and Bordaberry who, in an attempt to discredit Ferreira Aldunate, alleged that he had instigated a military coup against the president.[27]

The third and final crisis bringing about the *autogolpe* was instigated by the army's demand to punish a left-wing ex-Blanco, Senator Erro, accused of protecting terrorists. In the first two cases, the army managed to weaken President Bordaberry's support from his own party, thereby placing him at the mercy of the military. In the third stage, once the government was under its control, the military attacked the left-wing opposition, presupposing the apathy of the traditional parties. Simultaneously, they managed to remain on speaking terms with left-wing controlled organizations.

The reaction in Parliament, however, was met by a strong majority, profoundly antagonistic to the military's ultimatum. The larger Blanco faction, represented by Senator Dardo Ortíz, joined the Frente Amplio, claiming that the head of the intelligence service of the army, Colonel Ramón Trabal, attempted to force his arrest. Ortíz charged that the declarations of the imprisoned former Tupamaro, Amodio Pérez, incriminating Erro lacked credibility and were extracted under torture.

In general, the accused congressmen reacted erratically against the military, sometimes preemptively attacking them, while at other times becoming defensive. A year before the *autogolpe*, the General Assembly still expressed its confidence in "the constitutionalistic role of the Armed Forces."[28] However, when Jorge Batlle Ibáñez was arrested, Senator Vasconcellos stated that "this country is not made for having the military rule outside the constitutional framework."[29] The same senator in February 1973 precipitated the crisis by reading a document, alleged to have been circulated amongst Army officers, conspiring a military takeover.[30] In the following months, the parliamentary reaction to the exposure of their corruption was to minimize their benefits, and to counteract it by stressing the privileges granted to the military. Bari Gonzáles, of the progovernmental Blancos, denounced illegal loans to the military and their exclusive right to be exempted from the meat ban,[31] while Jorge Batlle exposed their tax-free cars and long-term payments for housing.[32] Blanco member Ferreira Aldunate again clearly repudiated the military's behavior and declared his resistance to their interventionist trends.[33] Furthermore, the left-wing opposition throughout this period accused the military of continuing the practices of torture of prisoners, indiscriminate arrests, and repressive measures covered by the emergency law.[34] Among the most outspoken was Senator Erro, who aroused the army's hostility by such denunciations in the very early stages.

Parliamentary support for the president was reduced drastically with the adoption of his submissive line, as seen in the reluctant attitude of Parliament toward the renewal of the state of emergency. After the army's accusation against parliamentarian corruption on March 31, after an hour of debate, Congress extended the state of emergency for 60 more days by a 65–63 vote. By June 1973, only his own Colorado reelection group, a few Blanco "*acuerdistas*," and even fewer extreme right-wing Colorados supported Bordaberry. The nonacceptance of the army's ultimatum of lifting parliamentarian immunity from Senator Erro and suggestions of alternative solutions for Erro's trial were connected to the fear of establishing a precedent which could be used against any congressman, no matter what his political orientation. It thereby created, for the first time, a coalition of the majority of the Houses in confrontation which an intransigent military. Moreover, it became a struggle for prestige, in which a retreat by the army could entirely change the image of their being all-powerful and the undisputed leaders of the nation.

On the eve of the dissolution, the passionate speeches were, for the liberals, mainly a war cry against the army, although Bordaberry, considered a tool in their hands, was also denounced as "the enemy of his people."[35] For the "1,001" list left-wing senators, however, all criticism focused on opposing a policy of impoverishment, corruption, torture, and violations by the president and the "clique of latifundist, meat industry, the clique of the swindling bankers," or the "economic power of the oligarchy,"[36] but not a single word was uttered against the army's behavior.

It is interesting to note that the executive decision to dissolve Congress was justified by Bordaberry in one of the most legalistic of arguments. Quoting articles of the United States Constitution, the old Spanish law system of the fourteenth century, French constitutional law, and world famous jurists,[37] he attempted to legitimize, by democratic norms, the *autogolpe*. During most of the crisis leading to the takeover, the process was characterized by legalistic disputes (resignation of ministers, questioning in Parliament, interpretation of the Constitution, and conflict of jurisdiction between the executive and the legislative, etc.). The efforts to bridge the legitimization gap with the project for constitutional reform and the creation of the "Council of State" are clear evidence of the importance in the Uruguayan tradition of democratic norms, one of the few obstacles toward an open and unrestricted absolutist military rule.

After the *autogolpe*, many parliamentarians of the opposition managed to escape. Ferreira Aldunate, Zelmar Michelini, Gutiérrez Ruiz, and others had to join Erro in Buenos Aires. Many political leaders of the Blanco party and the Frente Amplio were imprisoned, the former released after a few weeks and the latter, as in the case of Liber Seregni and the Communists, remained in prison most of the time until the present.[38]

The President

One can pinpoint two interrelated points of weakness in President Bordaberry, the first concerning his personality and the second, institutional. In a country where *"caudillismo"* is part of an historical tradition, the charisma of the political leader is a determining factor of his power base. Popular support has to surface not only in the voting figures, but also in a moment of crisis. In Bordaberry's case, during the dramatic process of confrontation with the military during the February crisis, when sources of strength became vital both for the military and for the president, only one to two hundred people came to the Presidential House to express solidarity with his person or with what he represented in the institutional system.[39] His complacent image was, to a large extent, a serious handicap, particularly when compared to the strong and authoritarian personality of his predecessor, although for some he did project a positive middle-class, family-oriented image.

In fact, he was never considered a first-rate candidate, but a pallid vice-presidential candidate of the Unión Colorado Batllista leader, Pacheco Areco. Organized as a reelectionist front, they first fought to win the referendum preceding the 1971 elections aimed at amending the Constitution in order to afford their presidential candidate a second term in office. In the eventuality that this amendment would not receive an absolute majority, as was later the case, Bordaberry's candidacy was the alternative. Bordaberry was not a veteran Colorado; he came from another small group, the landowner-led Ruralist faction, cooperating as a conservative wing in most previous regimes. In the Pacheco Areco administration, he served as minister of agriculture and was known as an obedient and docile friend. When Pacheco Areco's reelection was not permitted, the first impression was that the regime would continue to be run indirectly by Pacheco, with Bordaberry fulfilling the loyal duty of a "puppet president." However, the possibilities of *"Pachequismo"* were counteracted by a quick army move, in which Pacheco Areco and some of his relatives were exposed as being involved in illicit economic activities. His absence from the country and the critical rumors about his life-style in Spain undermined all of Pacheco Areco's power and influence over Bordaberry.

The second factor, the institutional framework, is also important, for if not for the nature of the electoral system, Bordaberry would not have been elected as a majority president. As can be seen in Table 5, he received a smaller number of votes than the major Blanco leader Ferreira Aldunate.

If we add to Ferreira Aldunate's personal success the fact that the Colorado electoral victory was based on a narrow margin of 10,000 votes, with the Frente Amplio opposition receiving 19 percent of the vote, the precarious situation of the elected president is largely explained.[40] His need for a coalition with at least

Table 5
Results in 1971 National Elections

Colorado Candidates		Blanco Candidates		Frente Amplio
Juan Bordaberry	325,246	W. F. Aldunate	383,113	(one candidate)
Dr. J. Batlle	217,344	Gral. M. Aguerrondo	201,452	Liber Seregni
A. Vasconcellos	44,437			
Gral. J. Ribas	8,381			
Total	595,408		584,865	271,339

some of the Blanco factions was not only in order to continue the participationist tradition, but out of the need to form a majority in Parliament.

Furthermore, the Cabinet's instability was outstanding. The sequence of ministerial resignations that occurred stemmed either from a refusal to accept the president's concessions to the army or because of the army's vetoing the appointment, especially in the defense portfolio, in which five successive ministers served during a period of ten months. In some cases, presidential genuflection to the army's *diktats* against parliamentarian leaders (Batlle and to a lesser extent Vasconcellos) inevitably struck against those lists participating in or supporting the coalition.

Throughout the crisis, one sees a gradual presidential acceptance of sharing power with the military, eventually ending in his total submission to them. It is interesting to note that the sudden change can be pinpointed during the second crisis, when he changed his attitude toward the military within a few days. In his letter of February 2 to Senator Vasconcellos, the president stressed:

> I cannot accept, therefore, under any circumstances, your assessment as to the existence of a movement which aimed to displace legality and counted upon the complicity and passivity of the Armed Forces and the President of the Republic. I can assure you that if somebody will come to the madness of thinking the contrary, the President of the Republic and the Armed Forces who are loyal to what he represents, will reaffirm by deeds the implicit will in their duties of singling out the responsibility of any one who will threaten the 'historic fact' of the existence of the political institutions.[41]

Yet, twelve days later, after conceding to the military, President Bordaberry announced in a public speech:

> The Armed Forces, who have repeatedly shown testimony of a great

spirit, of a great capacity, could not stay away from national life, because of its anxieties and pains, its hopes and sacrifices . . . . I always thought so from the beginning of my administration . . . . Today I can announce that following this thought, the Executive will create the appropriate institutional ways for the participation of the Armed Forces in the national task, within the framework of law and the Constitution.[42]

It seems that for a short period at the beginning, Bordaberry considered the possibility of remaining in power without making significant concessions to the army. The October crisis terminated with his acquiescence in replacing a minister, but the February crisis only ended when instruments were established to perpetuate military domination in civilian life through COSENA, the civilian-military National Security Council. From that time on, coupled with losing a parliamentary majority, the president surrendered to the army, excluding his objection to the lifting of immunity rights of old personal and political friends. He served as a civilian stamp that legitimatized the arbitrary demands of the military.

In fact, the rest of Bordaberry's administration strongly confirms his submissive attitude toward the military. There is only one exception, towards the end of his mandate in 1976, when he suggested to the army his continuation in power and the abolition of the political parties. For this deviation he was to pay very dearly, as it forced his early resignation.

Former Senator Julio M. Sanguinetti appropriately wrote: "We are in a dictatorship without a dictator. Bordaberry is not the harsh, authoritarian and impulsive man that overflows the constitutional restrictions and initiates with a Caesar-like will to exercise power on a personal basis."[43]

Senator Ferreira as stressed in the Foreword, develops two additional and perhaps contradictory explanations as to how the president paved the way for military intervention: firstly, he apparently developed a deepening aversion to Parliament, reacting to the disrespect and neglect shown him by many of the more prestigious and professional politicians. Furthermore, the continuous blocking of his policy by both Parliament and the army, albeit in contending directions, precipitated Bordaberry's choice to rely on the stronger. But the army's mounting strength in itself resulted from the mishandling of the presidential policy towards the military. This Ferreira considers to be the major explanation for intervention. An army unable to confront any of Uruguay's powerful neighbors, the ranking officers unreasonably outnumbered the troops' requirements. It was precisely this excess that traditionally allowed the president to select those who were to remain in active service and in top positions. Only about five percent of them had a direct control of the troops stationed in the different camps, and it would not have been a major problem for Bordaberry to station loyal elements in the more central positions. In the past, presidents never hesitated to make use of their legal powers and make sure that a third of those generals promoted by selection (the other two-thirds were promoted by seniority and competition) were among his supporters. Bordaberry dismantled this check-and-balance system; he even agreed to ask for the army's approval of the appointment of the chiefs of police, a right that had been previously exercised by the president, thereby shuttering the independence of the Policy, a force that in domestic affairs could not be disregarded as an element nearly as important as the armed forces themselves.

THE TUPAMAROS AND COMPETING MILITARY ORGANIZATIONS

In the period immediately preceding the three crises under focus, the MLN (Movement of National Liberation), Tupamaros, appears to have been connected with the rise of militarism in Uruguay. At this time, the conditions justifying and pushing the generals to military intervention were created.

The origins of the Tupamaros are traceable to 1962, when Socialist Rául Sendic attempted to organize a sugarcane workers strike and hold a protest rally in Montevideo.[44] Since then, sporadic acts of terrorism, distribution of propaganda, and "expropriations"[45] have been reported, but it was with the failure of the rural guerrillas and of Ché Guevara in Bolivia in 1968, that the urban guerrilla movement launched their full-scale activity. They disclosed the illegal economic activities in which the political elite was in one way or another connected, as in the case of the publication of the accounts of "Financiera Monty"; stressed the oppressive role of the United States by showing its involvement in repression through the capture of U.S. police expert Dan Mitirone and other officials; attempted to weaken the regime's image by exposing its impotency through guerrilla actions with the takeover of the Pando town for several hours and the two-time kidnapping of political and economic elite member Pereyra Reverbel; and ridiculed the leadership—as in the publication of photos of President Pacheco Areco shaving in the nude.[46] They also worked at dissuading the police from acting against the guerrillas by killing some when the armed forces joined the antiinsurgency action—as in the assassination of Police Inspector Héctor Morán Charquero, shot dead in his car; tried to elicit a greater consciousness for a more just society by distributing "expropriated" goods in slums and making certain that the San Rafael Casino was reimbursed of some of its stolen money so as to pay the salary of its employees; and attempted to precipitate a conflict situation, taking into account the geopolitical situation of Uruguay by involving it in a conflict with Brazil—as in the kidnapping of the Brazilian consul in Montevideo, Aloysio Dias Gomide.

President Pacheco Areco's mounting obstacles in taking action against the

Tupamaros led to the decision in September 1971 (decree 566/971) to involve the armed forces in the suppression of the guerrilla activities. By then, however, the Tupamaros had agreed to a truce, in order not to undermine the Frente Amplio's chances in the November national elections by creating a climate which might have frightened people from voting for any left-wing movement. Although skeptical as to the chances of achieving power through electoral means, the Chilean example of Allende's victory was sufficient to persuade the MLN to accept a temporary halt in their activities. However in March 1972, once President Bordaberry was elected and installed in power, the Tupamaros more vigorously renewed their activities. This time though, they had to face two additional forces, the counterguerrilla movements and the armed forces.

As for the former, the same groups reappeared on various occasions under different names: Movimiento de Restauración Nacional (MRN, Movement of National Restoration); Defensa Armada Nacionalista (DAN, National Armed Youth); Commando Armando Leses; Brigadas Nacionales (National Brigades); Juventud Uruguaya de Pie (JUP, Uruguayan Youth "Stand Up"); Comando Caza Tupamaros (CCT, Commando Tupamaro's Hunt). In addition, the existence of a Brazilian type "Death Squad" (paramilitary organization) was confirmed by Parliament.[47] On many occasions, counterguerrilla activities were even connected to police and army figures.[48] Furthermore, the coalition of Ruralist and right-wing and even President Bordaberry did not hide their sympathy towards the JUP leaders.[49]

The counterguerrillas did not confine themselves to fighting only Tupamaro members. On the contrary, the difficulties involved in identifying its members led them to act against any left-wing element connected with the Frente Amplio, or reportedly sympathetic to socialist ideas.[50] However, the use of violence by the counterguerrillas remained marginal, especially if compared with the intensive activities of the Tupamaros. Nevertheless, it was significant enough to create a fear of an expanding civil-war situation.

As for the armed forces, the Tupamaros' attempt to "dissuade" them by assassinating its members produced the opposite effect. The killing of frigate Captain Ernest Motto was described by a former Colorado minister as the action that "unleashed the undeclared civil war."[51] Furthermore, the assassination in July 1972 of Colonel Artigas Alvarez, the brother of the powerful commander of the army-police joint forces, General Gregorio Alvarez, only exacerbated the feelings of the military elite.[52] It created a climate among the upper echelons of the military that they too were vulnerable, and that the only way out was to act with speed and strength. Accordingly, some Tupamaro leaders who had previously escaped from prison were recaptured. Because of wretched torturing, they disclosed the whereabouts of their printing house, the "People's Prison," and names of key network members who were later killed or imprisoned. By September 1972, with the capture of Raúl Sendic, the Tupamaros were effectively finished. About 2,000 were held imprisoned in the Libertad prison, and the repressive apparatus that had already been effectively mounted then proceeded to harass other political forces, amongst which the nonviolent pro-Soviet Communists became the main target. As for reported declarations about the resumption of Tupamaro and left-wing activities in general, they have yet to be confirmed by any concrete evidence,[53] even three years after the *autogolpe*.

In order to understand the rationale[54] of the guerrilla leaders, one must dissect some of their theoretical writings. One of the ideologists, Abraham Guillén, speaks of the limitations of urban guerrillas and the impossibility of such a movement being capable of taking power by military means from the regular army. Instead, the process is an indirect one, in which catastrophic conditions must be created to bring about the dissolution of political power. Again, this cannot be produced directly by a small guerrilla organization. It is more a kind of dialectic process; in the first stage, economic exploitation, hunger, high children's mortality rate, and the use of violence in such a way as it is not perceived by the people. The guerrilla movement has to act to produce a confrontation with the government, justifying its "revolutionary violence" by claiming to act on behalf of the oppressed majority. The third stage is the "manifest violence," in which the government's repressive attitude is universally seen through its use of torture, restriction of public liberties, assassination, and so on. This finally produces a popular outburst, the "popular violence," in which the masses paralyze the country's life and capture political power from the disintegrating elite.[55]

Regarding the Tupamaros' role in the process of the active military takeover, one must also consider other important aspects. Only after the challenge of the Tupamaros was suppressed did the military devote its accumulated energy to other aspects of society. There were rumors that the military jailers accompanied imprisoned Tupamaros out of jail to their secret places, where documentation incriminating illegal activities and stories of corruption by the economic and political elite were concealed. By July 1972, the army leaders already regarded it as their duty to struggle against illegal economic activities, and a few months later, against what they considered to be corrupt political party representatives.[56]

The guerrilla arguments concerning the social situation in Uruguay had important repercussions on the military. Although they had previously shown minimal interest in confronting such problems,[57] the speed and efficiency of the army eventually aroused in large sectors of the population an admiration for what had been formerly thought of as only a decorative parade-oriented armed forces.

Equally significant were the gradual restrictions placed upon public liberties. Under the guise of fighting terrorism, the Emergency Laws permitted the detention of individuals without habeas corpus; censorship prohibited reporting the Tupamaro name or its activities in the press. While it may have been difficult for the army to have encouraged such a restrictive regime to confront the representative system, it nevertheless facilitated the establishment of an operational basis for the future. In this way, the argument for antisubversive action continued until after the fall of the parliamentarian regime.[58]

In a sense, the use of "revolutionary violence" by the MLN legitimized the implementation of similar methods by the government; torture, indiscriminate killing, the illegal use of mass media, and so on began to be regarded as an accepted practice in political life. Furthermore, the efforts launched by the Tupamaros to produce evidence connecting the political elite with corruption indeed succeeded in focusing public criticism on the latter and mortally affecting their prestige. The military simply had to continue such revelations in order to bring about the total collapse of the politicians' reputation, which they did enthusiastically. It was no surprise, then, to find that the explanation for the dissolution of the General Assembly was the "Crises of Powers" (the legislative representative power).

The presence of right-wing paramilitary groups, although largely ineffective, enabled some sectors of the population to regard the military as a pacifying force, seeking to apply "law and order" to a situation in which the separation of the contending extremists was required to avoid further bloodshed and a civil-war situation. Although practically all efforts of the military were directed toward the Tupamaros, some publicity stunts, such as the temporary closing of extreme right-wing publications—linked to the paramilitary organizations and advocating the suppression of liberalism in Uruguay—depicted the army as playing a moderating role.

Simultaneously, the sporadic activities of other small left-wing guerrilla groups, such as the neoanarchist Organizacion Popular Revolucionaria 33, also provided a justification for the continuation of the antisubversive campaign, even when the Tupamaros were considered to be totally defeated.[59]

Finally, the very existence of the guerrilla movement supplied the army with a rationale for curtailing legislative power. Senator Erro was accused of cooperating with the Tupamaros, on the basis of the confession of a tortured guerrilla leader.[60] The unwillingness of a congressional majority to subject Erro to military justice, and the decision that he should be judged by his own parliamentary colleagues, presented the army with a justification for establishing themselves as the only center of power. It is quite obvious that the dynamic and escalating process that pushed the military away from inertia and apathy did not stop with the extermination of the Tupamaro movement.

In conclusion, the role played by the Tupamaros in accelerating and perhaps even initiating military intervention in Uruguay was highly significant. Not only because they provided an excuse for the army's intervening in a state of internal turmoil and subversion, but also because in reality there was no alternative. This confrontation proved traumatic for a country where violence had all but disappeared from political life, barring the honorable duels. What is even more important, as will be discussed in the chapter dealing with the generals' perceptions, is that this phenomenon was acutely perceived by the army. Starting from a feeling of inner weakness and stagnation, when facing a dynamic and well-trained Tupamaro military counterpart, the army was forced to revive itself and overcome the great psychological barrier of becoming involved in a situation whose outcome was not clearly in its favor. One thereby witnesses a complete personality change, projecting a new image to others and to themselves.

INTEREST GROUPS

In this section, we shall discuss the trade union movement and its main organization, the Convención Nacional de Trabajadores (National Workers Federation, CNT), including approximately 90 percent of all Uruguayan workers; and university students and their representatives, the Federación de Estudiantes Universitarios del Uruguay (FEUU). These two groups were associated with the left-wing political parties represented in the Frente Amplio and constituted its major political support. We shall also analyze the respective influence of the Catholic church, the press, and rural groups. The army, as was stated beforehand, will be dealt with separately as the decision-making unit.

Frente Amplio: University and Trade Unions

The reunification of all the Marxist groups, the Christian Democrats, and splinter groups of both the Colorado and Blanco traditional parties into one single Popular Front was considered a great success for the old Communist party. In light of the encouraging results of the 1970 elections in Chile, some public opinion polls in Uruguay forecasting its first place,[61] and the Frente Amplio's massive meetings in Montevideo,[62] the results of the 1971 elections were disappointing. While in absolute terms, 19 percent of the vote represented a reasonable increase in their electoral force, the electoral way to socialism remained open, but with a difficult and distant process. Furthermore, while the Tupamaros accepted a cease-fire in order to permit the Frente Amplio to most optimally handle the electoral campaign, with the defeat, dedicated left-wing groups had to seek new means. For example, in other countries such as Peru, the Communists came out in support of a reformist nationalistic army regime. It was therefore quite feasible in Uruguay for those who were, at any rate, skeptical about the electoral system, and even for some democrats of the left, to seriously consider the possibility of reinforcing the reformist-nationalistic trend within the Uruguayan army. According to List 15, Colorado member Julio Maria Sanguinetti, "the Uruguayan left—especially the Communist, Socialist and Christian Democrat—encouraged the military advance, believing it was possible that the progressive tendencies hardly appearing will get stronger."[63]

Moreover, among the components of the Frente Amplio, some small but active groups, such as the Movimiento Revolucionario Oriental (MRO), were altogether skeptical of the electoral option, and both the military or the Tupamaro alternative represented for them the possible impetus for rapid change.

In the February 1973 crisis, Communiques Four and Seven published by the army were cited as evidence of such a growing reformist-nationalistic trend. The left-wing reaction was to condemn Bordaberry as a representative of the oligarchy, calling for the unity of the people, "understanding that the people include all its sectors, civil and *military* [my italics], secular and clerical, workers and university professionals...."[64] On February 17, the Frente Amplio's Presidential candidate presented a sympathetic analysis of the role of the military in politics. In claiming uniqueness for the Uruguayan process, he quoted army spokesmen in a refusal to return to "stages already overcome" or "becoming the strong-arm of economic or political groups."[65]

In the crucial days in March, the military's charges against the corruption of the legislators remained unanswered by the Frente Amplio, in spite of the fact that the attack was directed against all the politicians. The CNT and FEUU remained silent[66] and concentrated their efforts against President Bordaberry, demanding his resignation.

The decline in the general political situation, coupled with the systematic persecution of the left by the army, as personified in the attempt to arrest the Frente Amplio's Senator Erro, forced the Communists to seek an alliance with the liberal opposition. First Secretary Rodney Arismendi called for the "unity of the majority of the people to draw the country outside the abyss," praising similar declarations of ex-Commander in Chief Cesar Martinez, and of Blanco leader Wilson Ferreira Aldunate.[67] However, at the same time, there was no criticism of the military, only against the "oligarchy, this clique continuously enriching itself at the expense of the country, and holding power."[68] In this way, the Communists were trying to keep the two options open.

When only five days prior to the *autogolpe* a general strike was organized, the CNT limited its political demands of urging the military to bring about Bordaberry's resignation and calling for an increase in workers' salaries, "in the spirit of Army Communiques Four and Seven."[69] Typical of a well-organized trade union movement, it continued to emphasize as its main targets salary revindications and other concrete measures so as to prevent the deterioration of the workers' standard of living. Although this was the basic trend among the left, some groups nevertheless remained critical of the collaborationist line with the army. The Tupamaros, for instance, repeatedly refused to delude themselves about the progressive character of the military. They vocalized their disagreement with the Communist view, as an exiled source explained:

> True, we had had conversations with the military during last year, the first time in order to establish a truce that would enable us to gain time, and the

second time with the so-called nationalistic officers. We do not deny the importance of political work inside the Armed Forces, particularly among low-rank officers and soldiers, but we consider it a State institution aimed in the last resort to defending capitalism. There cannot be a better example than in Chile. In any case, the Armed Forces became a fresh political power, a reserve of the old degenerate classes, needed in order to perpetuate a dying system.[70]

Marcha, a very influential weekly of the left, also went out of its way to clarify that army involvement in politics was a negative phenomenon, stressing that a bad constitution was preferable to no constitution at all.[71]

The military's strategy towards the left was twofold: to encourage a rapprochement as far as economic demands were concerned, but to prevent its gaining any political power. During the first October crisis, "the Armed Forces made it clear to the Government that they considered the Trade Union demands to be justified and would not repress strikes [over wage increases]."[72] Yet when the CNT organized the strikes in March and emphasized its demand for Bordaberry's resignation, the armed forces "rejected the CNT's demands and announced that the Trade Unions should not engage in politics but limit their activities to labor wage questions."[73] A month later, an army spokesman, though recognizing some shared objectives with the CNT, declared that "the ways sustained by both our institutions are not reconcilable."[74] The dissolution of Parliament was accompanied by an immediate announcement of wage increases,[75] but at the same time, Bordaberry announced "the rejection of any ideology of Marxist origin that will try to use our difficulties, that will attempt to profit from our generous demanding and introduce herself as a saving doctrine and end as an instrument of totalitarian oppression."[76]

The day after the *autogolpe*, the CNT declared a general strike. Although the Communists apparently meant to hold only a 24-hour strike, the general repudiation of the coup by the 500,000 strong Trade Union Movement led to an unlimited one.[77] Through the minister of the interior, Colonel Bolentini, the military agreed to a slight increase in salary, less than half of what the workers had demanded, and called for an end to the strike and the opening of negotiations. Without suspending the strike, the CNT began negotiations with the government, but their political demands were rejected.[78] In the meantime, almost all of the left-wing political parties were banned, many of the Frente Amplio legislators jointed Senator Erro in exile; some were arrested, such as the left-wing military, Víctor Licandro, Carlos Zufriategui, Socialist ex-Congressman Cardozo, Colorado member H. Batalla, and later General Seregni and others.

In the first days of July, the government threatened the striking workers with dismissals and military mobilization if they did not return to work. When the negotiations failed, the CNT was declared illegal, and after fifteen days the strike collapsed. Late in July, the government passed a law, the "Guarantee of Labor," by which all political activities by the trade unions were forbidden, and the ability to declare strikes was severely limited.[79] It therefore took the army less than one month following the *autogolpe* to dispose with the organized left as a political factor. Eventually, the trade union's upper and middle-level leaders came to be found in El Cilindro, a prison in a former sports stadium.

Paradoxically, while the university represented the most active center of the both violent and nonviolent extreme left, the army generals disposed of this group last, a few months after the *autogolpe* and only after the other potential sources of opposition were brought under control. A partial reason may be that when pragmatically evaluating the real strength of this pressure group, the military did not assign to them a high priority. On the other hand, once its other opponents were neutralized, the army could have then tried to use other slower and more dissuading methods to depoliticize the university.

Since the sixties and perhaps even prior to them, there was a general feeling that political activism in the university overwhelmingly exceeded any accepted standards. In 1968, the minister of defense requested an investigation of high ranking army officers, including the general inspector of the army, General Liber Seregni, who was to later become the presidential candidate of the left. One finding was that "the offices of the student organizations of the different faculties constitute such a nucleus that, since it cannot be controlled by the University authorities, allows itself to undertake subversive activities. Also, some university organizations have been used as a center for aggression and as places of refuge for those for illegal activities, serving as storage for materials used for the disruption of the public order."[80]

Arms were found, bombs repeatedly exploded, memorials were held for student guerrillas killed in action, and teaching activities were barely able to continue. The political polarization of the student activists made clashes between extreme left and right-wing groups a normal scenario. Although the Communists managed to control the National Student Union (FEUU), nobody seemed able to put any order into the agitated atmosphere of the university.

The organization of right-wing student groups and its periodic incursions into the left-wing student premises provided the police with an excuse with which to enter the university in order to separate the opposing forces. In these raids, names of Tupamaro sympathizers fell into the hands of the police. On the other hand, one can assume that student activity outside the university was no longer felt in the months preceding the *autogolpe*. During this period, the government sent primary and secondary pupils on a long holiday and FEUU sympathizers took over and entrenched themselves in the university without being molested. In the first days of July, the university authorities declared themselves opposed to the dictatorship;[81] but for a long time, as long as the students did not leave the university grounds, political activity was tolerated.

The government felt that there might be a "silent majority" within the university that supported the government but had not made its feelings known, and they ordered a compulsory and secret election of university authorities. The groups corresponding to the Frente Amplio and other groups from left to right of center in opposition to the ruling party won an overwhelming victory in September 1973.

During the summer and autumn, the university organized public lectures analyzing the socioeconomic and legal situation of Uruguay, which had been steadily and seriously deteriorating, and tried to present solutions to this major national crisis. The newly elected university authorities were due to take office on October 29, 1973. On October 27, a bomb exploded in the Faculty of Engineering and killed a student, Marcos Caridad Jordán.[82] There are contradictory versions as to his role there. The Uruguayan authorities claim that he was making the bomb. One of his teachers, the ex-rector of the university, said that he found it hard to believe that Jordan was anything other than a serious and conscientious student. As a consequence of Jordan's death, the rector of the university, the deans of all faculties (and, instead of two deans who happened to be out of the country that weekend, the interim dean and an ex-dean) were all arrested,[83] as were some other members of staff and students. The rector and deans were held for nearly two months and questioned about their responsibility for the "Marxist infiltration" in the university and its having become a "center of subversion." The intervention in the university was officially declared.[84]

A large scale expulsion of university staff took place; the *depuración* was formalized by a decree which obliged all staff to pledge an oath against "Marxism" and in defense of the present regime.

Economic Pressure Groups:
The Middle Class and Ruralists.[85]

Most of the working strata were represented by the CNT, whose role has already been explored as a political and economic force. In Uruguay, the middle class forms the broadest stratum of the society, in contrast to other Latin American countries, and the liberal regime of the Colorados traditionally represented, to a greater extent, the urban middle class in politics.[86] The Blanco party was based more on the rural landowners, conservative groups, and the lower strata in the countryside and Montevideo. If there was indeed a connection between the political system and the economic group in power, one can say that the restrictions on representative democracy in Uruguay reduced the level of participation of the middle class in the country's political elite.[87]

The deteriorating economic stability and the atmosphere of terror and violence provoked by the urban guerrillas produced consternation among the middle classes. This was reflected in an increasing emigration to neighboring countries, a decline in political activity, and a loss of confidence in the established and traditional patterns of political life in Uruguay. Many of those in either direct or indirect contact with the public administration, public enterprises, or liberal professions, were alarmed by the imprisonment of friends and colleagues for illegal economic activities. This not only deterred them from involvement in dubious propositions, but frightened them into doing only what was necessary to maintain their personal position. The developed "spoil system" in public administration did not imply the dismissal of members of the outgoing administration, but rather the addition of civil servants from the new party in power. It made one functionary related to and dependent on others, and increased the fear that by indirect allegiance to a certain person, one's own future was threatened. These elements caused the managerial sectors to avoid "looking for trouble" and not to oppose the ascent of the military forces.

The analysis of political allegiance in the countryside is quite complex. On the one hand, one finds the Federación Rural (Rural Federation) which traditionally represented the upper sectors, the oligarchy of cattle growers. On the other hand, the Liga Federal de Accion Ruralista (Federal League of Ruralist Action), which was originally a more popular faction, initially attempted to control the Federación and later became a rival organization. Launched by a very successful radio commentator, Benito Nardone (nicknamed Chicotazo), he had a tremendous appeal with the lower and middle rural classes. Using a very simplistic argument that the people of the land were forced to support the "parasites" of the city and spouting strong anti-communist slogans, this faction became crucially important as a pivotal force which could decide the electoral victory of either the Colorado or Blanco party. Juan José Gari, Domingo Bordaberry and his son, the future president, belonged to this group. They signed a pact with the Blanco candidate Herrera who became president in the 1958 elections, and supported Colorado Pacheco Areco in the following elections, assuring his triumph. A rather opportunistic organization, its power nearly vanished after the death of Chicotazo, the charismatic leader.

We have already analyzed how Bordaberry was elected to the highest office as a consequence of Pacheco's failure to obtain reelection. In any event, the landowner-led Liga supported him while the more established Federación maintained connections with the Blanco party and as such was not keen in transferring its loyalties to the other side, continuing to show support to democratic and civil symbols even after the *autogolpe*. Taken as a class, however, the ruling circles surrounding President Bordaberry belonged to the conservative "oligarchy" of landowners, with an estimated 600 families,[88] large stockholders, and managers of banks, large corporations, and financial institutions. Although there were, in many cases, family relationships between these two groups, there were also social elements that joined the ranks of the upper class during times of social and economic mobility, or through party affiliations.[89] Uruguay's economic structure and foreign trade were primarily

based upon cattle and agriculture; therefore, these sectors continued to dominate during the twentieth century, becoming an important consideration in the
formulation of economic policy. Social agitation in the country and the instability of world prices encouraged them to strengthen their ties with the governing
circles, especially since Bordaberry himself had personal rural interests to
defend. In spite of the rise in prices and the decrease in income within the
salaried sector, the year 1972 represented, according to the Institute of Economy of the National University, "the period of the most formidable accumula-
tion of wealth that has been concentrated in one country in so few hands. The
result is even more impressive if one takes into consideration that these funds
have been absorbed in the greater part by the reduced capitalistic group that
holds that agro-exporting sector."[90] During the 1970s, there was also involvement in several speculative operations and in smuggling cattle to Brazil.

Furthermore, after October 1972, the army decided to focus its investigation
on economic crimes in the sectors of foreign trade and the meat-packing
industry and their relation to illegal transactions in the private banking sector.[91]
Their linkages with officers of the Pacheco Areco administration and with some
politicians in Congress, at that time, allowed the military to bring into question
the prominence of the two groups; to the military's credit, there were certainly
sufficient instances in which guilt could be readily established.[92]

For the upper class, as well as for the Communists, the army was an unknown
factor. In the beginning, they were unsure whether to oppose or join forces with
them. However, after February 1973, the landowners decided to support the
military elite, hoping, as was eventually realized, that the more conservative
army faction would dominate.

The Church

Uruguay is perhaps the most secular of Latin American countries. The
separation between church and state, instituted by the liberal and anticlerical
Colorados at the beginning of the twentieth century, has become an accepted
practice, thus minimizing the influence of this force over the elected governments of Uruguay. Although the overwhelming majority of the population is
Roman Catholic, the rate of church attendance is low. "Religious observance
tends to be greatest among intellectuals and the working classes."[93]

Although a traditional Catholic party, Unión Civica, did exist, it did not play
a crucial role in political life until the end of the 1960s, when it gave birth to the
Christian Democratic party, adopted more progressive positions, and became
one of the pivots of the Frente Amplio. This development paralleled changes
among the church hierarchy. The social justice content of Christianity in the
Second Vatican Council (1962–65) was strongly supported by the church, from
the archbishop of Montevideo down to a great part of the clergy. What came to

be called the "*tercermundismo*," a Third World concept, and the "*concientizacion*," an awareness of the need for social change, became the position of the more active Uruguayan clergy, while the more traditional groups, linked to the upper class, remained on the defensive. The Uruguayan Bishop's Conference in 1969, which condemned the use of violence and torture by the police surrounding the *autogolpe*, maintained its stand, reaffirming that "it is not possible to hide the death, physical punishment and torture,"[94] executed by the government.

Another declaration of the Uruguayan Bishops' Conference in June 1972, while stressing that "as bishops, our sole motivation is of a pastoral character . . . the mission is religious and not political," expressed, nevertheless, a subtle criticism towards the government and the armed forces, as illustrated in two of the document's sixteen points:

> 7. We aspire to profound transformation in the country, inspired in the Christian conviction of our people and aimed at achieving a fraternal and solidary coexistence.

> 9. But we have been receiving a great number of coinciding testimonies related to the inhuman treatment given to some prisoners, who have been linked or not with subversive activities . . . . In connection with our ministerial duties and in the service of all men, we cannot remain silent when death, physical maltreatment, torture, and unjustified imprisonment constitute forms of a radical rejection of the dignity expected from a human being . . . .[95]

At the same time, although not categoric in the condemnation of guerrilla activities, they attempted to provide some justification for such actions of desperation:

> 3. It is in this context [the problems in the Uruguayan society] that the actions of armed groups operating outside the framework of law emerge in the country. We think, therefore, that the illegitimate resistance to change, the scepticism with regard to the future and the gravity of injustice, appear to be some of the motivations of those who began subversive activities in the country.[96]

As can be expected, the less dependent political life became on the political parties and the democratic rules of the game, the more a traditionally-established institution, such as the church, could become a vehicle for expression of political ideas.

When important prelates such as Montevideo Archbishop Monsignor Partelli showed an unwillingness to grant legitimacy to and cooperate with the military regime, it attempted to pressure the church into adopting a docile attitude.[97]

General Forteza included the Uruguayan church as one of the centers that had been subverted by international Communism and "whose ruinous villainous and treasonous actions must be once and forever expurgated."[98] The dissonance created by the criticism of the high-ranking clergy in the minds of fervent Catholic adherents among the traditional ruling elite, such as Bordaberry himself, had a stronger effect than the church itself as a pressure group.

The Protestant church—which is even weaker than the Catholic church in Uruguay—has also been a target of government accusations. The evangelist publication *Mensajero Valdense* was closed in December 1974. The government advanced the following reasons:

> In its editorial column, the journal regularly published an article presenting the aims of the religious communities making up the World Council of Churches as economic aid to subversive Uruguayan, Chilean and Vietnamese groups, as well as such groups operating on African territory. The World Council of Churches is an international organism, based in Geneva, encouraging subversive activities on a worldwide scale, directed until 1972 by the Marxist, North-American C. Blake, Laureat of the Soviet award, the Lenin Prize, and presently directed by Philip Potter, who disseminates propaganda for chaos and anarchy as means to social change, invariably supporting Marxist subversion in the five continents and materially contributing to terrorist movements operating on an international scale.[99]

Arrested priests have not been spared the treatment reserved for political prisoners. In 1970, Father Pier Luigi Mugioni, a Jesuit priest, was arrested and severely tortured. He later testified: "They gave me so much *picana* (electric prod) that when I was transferred to Punta Carretas (the Montevideo prison), I still had the marks."[100] The report of the World Council of Churches' mission in 1972 mentioned among the prisoners held incommunicado and without trial three Methodist pastors and many Roman Catholic priests.

Mass Media and Public Opinion

With a ratio of 310 newspapers per 1,000 inhabitants,[101] Uruguay has been ranked at the height of worldwide newspaper circulations. For many years, nearly all the newspapers were dependent on the traditional parties,[102] but recently, those belonging to the left began to surface. Table 6 depicts the situation in 1970.[103]

The lack of an independent press has prevented the media from evolving into a "fourth power." Practically all ideas expressed have followed party lines, with no better chances of influencing the political process and public opinion than the parties themselves.

Table 6
Leading Uruguayan Newspapers, 1970*

Title	Estimated Circulation	Remarks
El Diario	55,000	Colorado Party; photographs, sports, news, entertainment
El Pais	35,000	Blanco Party (Beltran faction); conservative appeal
El Dia	30,000	Colorado Party (traditional Batllista founded);founded by Jose y Ordonez
La Manana	25,000	Colorado Party; progovernment
BP Color	25,000	Catholic Action; all color tabloid
Accion	15,000	Colorado Party (list 15 - Unity and Reform)
El Popular	12,000	Communist Party daily; Moscow line
Marcha	18,000	Leftist intellectual weekly

From 1968 on, the press began to suffer from partial censorship, and in 1969, a law was decreed forbidding the publication of subversive news and, among other things, the use of the name Tupamaros. For several days, dailies such as *El Debate* and *El Popular* were closed down as punishment, and the Socialist *El Sol* and *Epoca* were shut indefinitely. Censorship now existed, but it was still easy to express ideas opposing the government through more subtle and indirect means. Still, the growing resort to sanctions as a deterring measure is shown by the fact that the frequency of newspaper closings increased until some forty-four had occurred between 1967 and 1972.[104]

Following the *autogolpe*, restrictions grew more severe. The press was obliged to reproduce the text of official statements, and by a special decree passed at the end of June, they were forbidden to publish anything offensive to the regime or disturbing to public order and tranquility. All opposition newspapers were closed. (*Acción, El Popular*, the Christian Democratic *Ahora*, Frentist *Ultima Hora*, and *Marcha*). *Marcha* ironically used the headline "This is not dictatorship" to publish the list of restrictions declared by the government. It delved into the nineteenth century to quote texts of Artigas and other heroes, but in the end, it too was indefinitely closed.

On the other hand, during the years 1970–73, the right-wing press, which openly favored military involvement in politics, was strengthened.[105] The weekly *Nación* represented the right-wing collaborationist wing of the Blanco party, and the *Ninth of February* stressed support for the army leadership. *Azul*

Table 7
Public Opinion Poll

Opinion on Security Measures (Emergency Laws)

Beneficial to the country	33%
Not beneficial	58%
Don't know, no answer	9%

Opinion on detention without judge's approval

Favorable	11%
Unfavorable	69%

Opinion on prohibition of public meetings

Favorable	40%
Unfavorable	47%

Opinion on the attitude of the Army and Police towards recent developments (Killing of pro-guerrilla student Liber Acre)

	Army	Police
The attitude was correct	48%	26%
Not correct	24%	46%
Other answers	4%	18%
Don't know, no answer	24%	10%

Opinion on security measures according to social class

	Higher class	Middle class	Popular * class	Marginal+ class
Agreement with measure	41%	26%	35%	51%
Disagreement	59%	74%	65%	49%

* Popular class is defined as composed of clerks and classified and uncalssified workers

\+ Marginal stratum is defined as composed of domestic help (maids), soldiers, police without rank, and unemployed

y Blanco went so far in its criticism of liberalism that it repeatedly attacked President Bordaberry, often resulting in suspension of the publication. For instance, the following arguments are found in one of its editorials:

> Liberalism is atheist . . . . The liberal finds himself disarmed facing such a situation [of crisis]. The nation, because of the political party structure, instead of being united in the pursuit of the once common well-being, finds itself divided and with absolutely different aims, making it impossible to strive together, and in the crossroads of an economic and social crisis, the system totally fails, and will have to start again, but now with a totally new scheme . . . . Liberalism is corruption because it is incapable

of curbing it . . . . Liberalism places faith in institutions rather than in men, and the most elementary experience reveals the opposite.[106]

There are also seventy radio stations and nineteen television stations in Uruguay, mostly of a commercial nature, but in some cases also affiliated with political factions. They were less interested in politics and can be disregarded as a source of political influence. However, the military considered them an important means for the diffusion of their ideas. Lacking any organizational base within the civil population, they sought any possible means of establishing contact with the people, and broadcast many communiques appropriately phrased so as to attract the sympathy of large sectors of the population. The army was quite concerned about its popular image, and even in the February 1973 crisis, they considered the use of radio stations for broadcasting communiques to the people to be important. In its search for direct contact with the citizens, and when, following the *autogolpe*, most political parties were disbanded, the army used the slogan that "the worker is not alone." [107]

Conceivably, the attitude of the population to the military can be measured by public opinion polls. Unfortunately, data are available only for the years 1960-1968;[108] nevertheless, certain elements might be indicative of the general attitude in later stages.

The pursuit of corruption was also an activity that reinforced the popularity of the military. A poll published by the Instituto de Opinion Pública showed that 89 percent of the respondents believed that the government bureaucracy was corrupt and 88 percent believed that it should be dealt with severely. Sixty percent of those polled sympathized with the policies put forward by the military, and a similar percentage believed the country was headed for outright military rule.[109]

Although it would be difficult to reach clearcut conclusions from a few sporadic polls—which were allegedly of low reliability—it is interesting to underline two observations based upon the above mentioned figures: first, the army is undoubtedly more popular than the police; and second, support for the military is highest in the lowest sectors of the population, followed by the upper class, while the middle class is its strongest opponent.

Perhaps the popular feeling at the time of the *autogolpe* was best depicted in the description found in the *Wall Street Journal*: "Despite scattered opposition, it appears that most Uruguayans are resigned to the abridgement of their liberties. Many people seem to prefer stability (even on horseback) to turmoil and instability." [110]

NOTES

1. A thorough analysis is presented by Ronald H. McDonald, "Electoral Politics and

Uruguayan Political Decay," *Interamerican Economic Affairs* 26 (1972): 25–45.

2. According to one source, once the Colorado candidate for the 1958 elections, Luis Batlle Berres was defeated, a group of officers suggested plotting a coup in order to prevent the Blanco administration from taking over. Carlos G. Banales, "Función Política de las Fuerzas Armadas Uruguayas," in *Fuerzas Armadas, Poder y Cambio* (Caracas: Tiempo Nuevo, 1971), p. 254.

3. This was the fifth constitution in the twentieth century, preceded by those of 1917, 1934, 1942, and 1941. By reestablishing a one-man presidency by a majority vote, it still did not eliminate the support given to the idea of the *colegiado*.

4. For a general background, see Philip B. Taylor, *Government and Politics of Uruguay* (New Orleans: Tulane University Press, 1960).

5. For a comprehensive analysis of the internal and external causes of the economic crisis in Uruguay, see Jorge Irisity, "Uruguay: El fracaso de la opción neo-liberal," *Nueva Sociedad* (1975): 17–37.

6. *Facts on File*, September 2–8, 1973.

7. *La Opinión*, January 1, 1973.

8. Ibid., June 22, 1973. Another source points out that the Uruguayan government's economist analyst admitted that the GNP in 1969 was below the 1966 level and that the GNP per person was 12% less than in 1956. Thomas E. Weil et al., *Area Handbook for Uruguay* (Washington: American University, 1971), p. 272.

9. *La Opinión*, January 1, 1973. To this last figure, one must add the large numbers of head smuggled to Brazil through Uruguay's northern frontier.

10. Carlos A. Rama, *Sociología del Uruguay* (Buenos Aires: EUDEBA, 1965), p. 79.

11. *The Military Balance 1974-5* (London: International Institute for Strategic Studies, 1974), p. 67.

12. *Almanaque Mundial 1975* (Panama: Editorial América, 1975).

13. *El Cronista Comercial*, Buenos Aires, June 2, 1975.

14. Luis Marcadar, Nicolás Reig, and José Enrique Santias, "Una Economía Latino-americana," in *Uruguay Hoy* (Buenos Aires: Siglo XXI, 1971), p. 102.

15. *Facts on File*, December 9–15, 1973, p. 1047.

16. For a broader picture about the role of the traditional political parties, see Martin Weinstein, *Uruguay, the Politics of Failure* (Westport, Conn.: Greenwood Press, 1975).

17. Weil, p. 210.

18. Declaration of the Central Committee of the Herrerista Youth, *Azul y Blanco*, February 14, 1973.

19. *La Opinión*, March 26, 1973. Mentioned in a broadcast message of the armed forces (read by an officer in the presence of the commanders in chief of the three branches and other high-ranking officers).

20. *Azul y Blanco*, February 14, 1973.

21. *Clarín*, March 25, 1973.

22. *La Opinión*, March 25, 1973. Batalla was the target of allegations that he had communicated a government decision to devalue the peso to the press (an affair called the *"infidencia"*). However he was neither detained nor tried for such an offense. Instead he was subjected to the Military Justice and accused of "attempting to undermine the morale of the army" in a speech broadcast on radio and television in which he attacked Cristi, head of the First Military Region. He criticized the general for violating his constitutional and legal duty of not intervening in politics.

23. Ferreira considered that the weakening of the presidential power could produce a rupture in the constitutional order. *La Opinión*, October 24, 1972.

24. *Marcha*, May 17, 1973, p. 11.

25. Ibid., reproducing the text of Ferreira's intervention in the Senate.

26. *Marcha*, March 2, 1973, interview with Héctor Gutiérrez Ruiz.

27. *El País*, May 10, 1973.

28. Following a debate about a case of death under torture, the following text was adopted: "The House of Representatives expresses its confidence in the Armed Forces of the Republic, loyal to their unbroken historical tradition, will impose the fulfillment of the legal and constitutional norms that establish, in all circumstances, the respect of the dignity of the human being . . . ." *Diario de Sesiones de la Cámara de Representates* 609, June 22, 1972, p. 876. Debate on the death of the citizen Luis Carlos Batalla.

29. *La Opinión*, October 7, 1972.

30. A. Vasconcellos, *Febrero Amargo* (1973): 99–139. He would go on and say to the army that they should aim their threats elsewhere. *Facts on File*, April 1–17, 1973, p. 282.

31. *La Opinión*, March 25, 1973.

32. *La Opinión*, March 28, 1973.

33. *La Opinión*, March 29, 1973.

34. The left-wing press had consistently denounced such acts; see, for example, "Informe sobre Torturas," in *Cuestión* 17 (1972); and "Report of the Assassination of Ibero Gutierrez," in *Cuestión* 16 (1972).

35. *El Popular*, June 27, 1973. Quoted from Wilson Ferreira Aldunate's speech. Senator Vasconcellos, Hierro Gambardella, Paz Aguirre, Grauer, and others expressed themselves along similar lines.

36. Ibid., quoted from Senators Rodríguez Camusso and Enrique Rodríguez.

37. *Ultima Hora*, June 27, 1973.

38. In 1976, formal measures were taken to suppress the political rights of all former members of the parliamentary opposition for a period of fifteen years, thereby effectively bringing to its end this traditional institution.

39. Although the UPI reports about 500 persons demonstrating and a man in the crowd shouting "We will die for the President," (UPI cable *Jerusalem Post*, February 13, 1973), most sources consulted and personal enquires stressed precisely the opposite, the lack of enthusiasm of the people toward Bordaberry. In this particular crisis, more people were attracted by curiosity to see the barricades built by the navy in the old city area of Montevideo, and the day during which the demonstration in front of Bordaberry's house took place, football stadiums were filled, as usual.

40. These figures have been contested by Ferreira Aldunate's supporters, and the Blanco party as a whole, claiming that his victory over Bordaberry was by a higher margin.

41. A. Vasconcellos, p. 17.

42. "Siete Días que Conmovieron a Uruguay," in *Cuadernos de Marcha*, p. 42.

43. *La Opinión*, June 30, 1973.

44. For a detailed account of the MLN activities, see Alain Labrousse, Carlos A. Aznárez, and Jaime E. Canas, *Tupamaros, Fracaso del Che* (Buenos Aires: Orbe, 1969).

45. "Expropriation" in this context, means that money belonging to the government or private interest (banks, casinos, etc.) is stolen to be used for the benefit of the *Tupamaros*, or distributed among the people.

46. *La Nación*, February 28, 1972.

47. *Keesing's Contemporary Archives*, 25412, (1972). Statement of Héctor Gutiérrez Ruiz [Blanco], President of the Chamber of Deputies.

48. See José Pedro Púrpura's declarations of the Death Squad activities getting the agreement of certain police officers. *Cuestión* 17 (1972): 16–18. Armando Acosta y Lara, a former under-secretary in the Ministry of Home Affairs is mentioned among the founders of the Death Squads in Uruguay. His name and further evidence is disclosed in Geronimo Alsina, "Uruguay: la guerra y los Tupamaros," *Revista Latinoamericana* 29/30 (1972): 211–15.

49. Ibid., p. 25.

50. See report about the assassination of Ibero Gutiérrez in *Cuestión* 16 (1972): 16–19.

51. See article by Julio María Sanguinetti, *La Opinión*, July 24, 1973.

52. "This was the first time that the revolutionary organization [the Tupamaros] perpetuated such an act . . . . The Armed Forces are lamenting a wound in their own flesh. The very moment, so often predicted in the talks at the officers clubs ('the day that they attack one of us would be different'), this very day had then arrived . . . . For the first time, since the last civil war in 1904 the Uruguayan Army is living in a climate of war, with a real conscience, that only blood can create." *Clarín*, July 26, 1972.

53. *Le Monde*, July 29, 1973; *Clarín*, September 21, 1973; *La Opinión*, November 23, 1973.

54. On the ideological debate, see Edy Kaufman, "La Estrategia de las Guerrillas," *Problemas Internacionales* 20 (1973): 12–28.

55. Abraham Guillén, *Estrategia de la Guerrilla Urbana* (Montevideo: Manuales del Pueblo, 1966); and by the same author, *Desafío al Pentágono, la Guerrilla Latinamericana* (Montevideo: Andes, 1969).

56. The approach in three stages of antiguerrilla struggle, antieconomic illegal activities, and against the legislators is forwarded by Jorge Batlle's newspaper, *Acción*, June 27, 1973.

57. "What happened was perhaps, that in the compulsory study that the Army did on the subversion problem, it found out that it was treating more seriously the consequences than the cause and that there existed among the Tupamaros a primary outlook of rebellion against the many real evils of the fatherland: economic injustice, unjustified canonries; in other words, a series of evils that affect the small countries of our Latin America." Héctor Gutiérrez Ruiz, "Las Fuerzas Armadas y la Realidad del Pais," *Estrategia* 19/20 (1972/73): 28.

58. In March 1973, speaking in favor of the renewal of the emergency laws, Defense Minister Bolentini argued that, although the urban guerrilla movement was practically defeated, it should not be given an opportunity to reorganize. See *Facts on File*, April 1–17, 1973, p. 282.

59. *Clarín*, July 29, 1972.

60. It was Hector Amodio Perez, ons of the MLN leaders, who testified about his connections with Frente Amplio member Senator Erro; *Clarín*, May 9, 1973; *Clarín*, May 15, 1973. The whole episode remains unclear. Perhaps due to the application of extreme torture or for other reasons, Perez was willing to publish a book not only revealing information about the Tupamaros, but also incriminating the democratic politicians.

61. An unpublished poll of the Montevideo branch of the Gallup Institute assigned to the Frente Amplio 30% of the potential voters, 28% to the Colorados, and 22% to the Blancos. *Confirmado*, Buenos Aires, May 19, 1971. Apparently, the government was interested in magnifying the support given to the Frente and thereby creating the impression among the voters that there was only one choice: either the Colorados or Communism. To vote for the Blanco party would then be a "waste." The Frente also encouraged such a dichotomy from a totally different angle.

62. In one of the major electoral meetings in the history of Uruguay, on March 26, 1971, the Frente Amplio reported a 200,000 person attendance (more cautious estimates of the police gave 140,000). This of course encouraged optimism, but the final total votes collected by the Frente Amplio were only 271,339.

63. *La Opinión*, July 18, 1973.

64. *La Opinión*, March 27, 1973.

65. *Cuadernos de Marcha*, February 23, 1973, p. 45.

66. Ibid. Speaking about the conflict of the armed forces with the "most reactionary regime that our country has ever known," Seregni adds: "The oligarchy sacrifices its political expressions as obsolete and throws herself to seduce and conquer the Armed Forces, trying to turn them into their last card. But she [the oligarchy] feels insecure and worried. This is why she tries so hard. The Oligarchy is desperate about the new political concern of the Armed Forces given by the struggle against the subversion," pp. 45–50. The Communist slogan in April was, "The question is not between civilian and military, but between people and oligarchy, between honest and dishonest," *La Opinión*, April 13, 1973.

67. *El Popular*, June 27, 1973.

68. Ibid., p. 9.

69. *La Opinión*, June 29, 1973.

70. *Le Monde*, September 29, 1972.

71. In an issue published under severe censorship on June 30, 1973, a few days after the *autogolpe*, *Marcha* published texts of many previous editorials in which the danger of right-wing military takeover was consistently expressed.

72. *Keesing's Contemporary Archives*, 2569, January 22–28, 1973.

73. Ibid., 2598, July 16–22, 1973.

74. *Marcha*, June 30, 1973.

75. *El País*, June 29, 1973.

76. Ibid.

77. *La Opinión*, June 29, 1973.

78. The major CNT demands were: restoration of public liberties and constitutional guarantees; reestablishment of the rights of organized political parties and trade unions; linking of income to the cost of living index; agreement on a minimal basis of economic and social reforms; resignation of Bordaberry and the establishment of a provisional government; the organization of a popular referendum. *La Opinión*, July 6, 1973.

79. Strikes in essential public services were forbidden, the liberty of labor had to be respected when a strike was declared by the Trade Unions with no compulsory affiliation, conciliation committees prior to strike declarations, and other restrictions. *La Opinión*, July 25, 1973.

80. *Documentos*, Publicación Oficial Conjunta, Ministerio del Interior, Ministerio de Defensa Nacional, Ministerio de Educación y Cultura, November 24, 1973. This freely distributed tabloid includes not only the text of the intervention decree but a graphic account of what is given as evidence of clandestine activities, Marxist propaganda, Communist fund raising, disorder in the university functioning, etc.

81. The text follows similar lines to the Communist-inspired CNT demands. *La Opinión*, July 3, 1973.

82. *Facts-on-File*, December 9–15, 1973 p. 1046.

83. *Documentos*.

84. *Marcha*, November 1, 1973, p. 12.

85. The concept "ruralist," within the context of Uruguayan politics, defines the political force representing the interests of the landowners, controlling the agricultural and livestock fields of the country's economy.

86. A.M. Grompone, "Las Clases Medias en el Uruguay," (Washington: Unión Panamericana, 1960); and John J. Johnson, "The Emergence of the Middle Sectors," in *Latin American Politics*, ed. Robert D. Tomasek (New York: Anchor Books, 1966), pp. 169–96. A further confirmation is given in the results of a public opinion poll, showing that Colorado supporters among the Montivedeo middle class amounted to 39%, compared with 29% for the National party and 31% for the Frente Amplio. *La Mañana*, November 3, 1971.

87. Factors that had influence on this reevaluation of the economic crisis are the disintegration of the traditional political parties, the growing loss of the legitimacy of power, the gradual abandonment of the democratic-parliamentarian form of government, the radicalization and change of the level of the workers struggle and of wide sectors of public administration "employees, the incidence of the forms of armed struggle, etc." Gerónimo de Sierra, "Estructura Económica y Estructura de Clases en el Uruguay," in *Uruguay, Poder, Ideología y Clases Sociales* (Montevideo: Instituto de Ciencias Sociales, 1970), p. 148.

88. "The great majority of the productive land is held in large estates of over 2,500 acres, and is owned by the rural upper class. About one-fifth of this land is concentrated in the hands of a small number of families in estates over 12,500 acres, and an estimated 600 families control, directly or indirectly, one-third to one-half of the fertile land in the country," Weil, p. 70. In many

newspapers, the name of Jose Gari appears as a close associate of Bordaberry, linking the government with economic Uruguayan and North American circles. Benito Medero, one of the important ministers in Bordaberry's cabinet, also represented the ruralist sector and served as one of the major links between the government and it.

89. Carlos Real de Azúa, "Politica, Poder y Partidos Políticos en el Uruguay de Hoy," *Uruguay Hoy*, p. 190.

90. *La Opinión*, June 22, 1973. According to *Real de Azúa*, this process started already with the previous administration: "The Pacheco Areco administration seems to be more inclined than any other in the country—from Latorre to nowadays—to favor the higher economic sectors, less careful to fulfill the task of social compromise, which with all the preferences that it involucrates, was indeed the traditional work of the political power in Uruguay," *Real de Azúa*, pp. 189–90. While in 1972 the wages of the employed on the average went down 20%, the livestock holders increased their income from 41.416 miliion Uruguayan pesos to 100.020 million, which, even taking into account the rate of inflation, represented a fat share of the national profits. *Ultima Hora*, June 29, 1973.

91. *La Opinión*, October 24, 1972.

92. *La Opinión*, March 8, 1973. Among those incriminated of other economic crimes, we find the former Foreign Minister Peirano Facio (owner of the *Banco Mercantil*); the director of the Telephone Company (UTE), Pereira Reverbel; the former president himself, Pacheco Areco (in relation with transactions with the Spanish national airlines Iberia); Jose Gari, involved in a fantastic story of tax evasion. Other stories covered PLUNA, the small Uruguayan airlines; ANCAP, the national oil company; and the Montevideo City Council.

93. Weil, p. 164.

94. *Marcha*, June 16, 1972, p. 9; and *La Opinión*, November 23, 1973.

95. *Marcha*, June 16, 1972.

96. Ibid.

97. *La Opinión*, December 4, 1973.

98. The action of international Communism "has reached the Church itself, violating in this institution the rights and obligations that the State has granted to the different religions." *La Opinión*, September 29, 1973.

99. *Ici*, January 15, 1975.

100. Amnesty International, *Uruguay: The Position of the Churches*, (London, 1975).

101. *The New York Times Encyclopedic Almanac, 1970* (New York: Section Individual World Nations, 1970).

102. Instituto de Estudios Políticos para América Latina, p. 80.

103. Weil, p. 249.

104. From the total of forty-four closings, thirty-six were temporary and eight permanent. See table in Ronald H. McDonald, "The Rise of Military Politics in Uruguay," *Interamerican Economic Affairs* 28 (1975): 32.

105. *La Opinión*, December 9, 1973.

106. *Azul y Blanco*, February 14, 1973.

107. *El País*, July 4, 1973.

108. Data taken from the report of the Instituto de Ciencias Sociales on "La Opinión Pública en Montevideo", used by Enrique Carpena in "Clase Social, Ideología y Opinión Pública", in Instituto de Ciencias Sociales, *Uruguay: Poder, Ideología y Clases Sociales*, pp. 64–72.

109. *Latin America*, March 2, 1973.

110. *Wall Street Journal*, July 24, 1973.

4.
The Decision-Making Elite:
The Army Generals

Numbering 20,000 soldiers, the Uruguayan army, when compared to its population, is one of the largest on the continent. In addition, there are the departmental police and the maritime police[1] totaling 17,000 men, who after the second crisis in February, passively joined the army in its political moves. However, the army's strength is still insufficient to prevent aggression by either the Argentinian or the Brazilian armed forces.[2] Because of this, the military in Uruguay was for a long time seen as little more than a decorative force, the minimum required for a ''normal'' country; in fact, Uruguayans were proud of this comparative weakness, as it stressed the civilian character of the Uruguayan system.

In contrast to most Latin American countries, Uruguay's armed forces were not based on compulsory military service, but rather on a career army which provided its professionalism. The rank-and-file soldiers usually came from the lowest strata and together with the officers formed a close, introverted unit. At the top of the hierarchy were 12 generals and 125 subordinate officers[3] or, according to other sources, 21 generals.[4] The largest military branch was the army, which provided during the analyzed process the overwhelming majority of the decision-making elite. The high rate of rotation in leadership, particularly until the February crisis, was partially due to enforced retirement every two years of the two senior generals of each service, providing generous retirement provisions.

Nevertheless, the attraction of political life increased, particularly after General Gestido's presidency in 1966; by the time of our study, nearly every faction wanted to include a high-ranking officer within its leadership.

In order to portray the independence of civilian power, the 1967 Constitution

55

confirmed that the president was the chief of the armed forces and gave him the authority to decide about the promotion of new generals to Congress, as well as to retire any officer. However, the three branches were separately linked to the executive, and until 1970, lacked a coordinating body. Symptomatic of the changing army was the decision in 1970 to create the Junta de Comandantes with representatives from each of the three branches. Also, the absence of a chief of staff with jurisdiction over all the armed forces prevented the concentration of power in one hand, with decision making on a federated basis. The lack of a unifying force inside the armed forces was somewhat compensated for by the appointment of a minister of defense or interior who had previously served in the army or was associated with this body in other ways. In the period under consideration, the military forced the president to appoint their candidate, Colonel Bolentini (ret.), who became the link between the generals and the civilian rulers.

It is unrealistic to speak in terms of a military "caste" in Uruguay, for most of the officers came from the middle or lower-middle classes, and more than 50 percent from the rural areas.[5] The lack of prestige, low salaries, and negligible political corporative influence placed army officers on a relatively low social level. Although this image did not prove a sufficient incentive to sons of the Uruguayan elite, the possibility of rapid mobility was considered attractive by the lower sectors of society.

In harsh economic terms, the declaration of a state of emergency allowed the military to draw a double salary and provided an incentive for the prolongation of this exceptional measure. While in 1967 the salary of a primary school teacher was equal to one of a captain, by 1971 it barely reached the wage of a sergeant.[6] Other privileges were also acquired by the military, such as being exempt from meat rationing. These privileges were increasingly denounced in the Congress.[7]

One can gauge the extent of active military involvement by the beginning of the first crisis in October 1972, when 500 officers of the air force and army (the navy still very much under legalistic influence) met in the Military Center to discuss the pursuit of the investigation of economic crimes and the demand for the defense minister to resign.[8] In order to specify the military decision-making elite, we shall take into consideration not only those generals who remained in active service during the period of our study, but also those who retired, but maintained participation in politics through the political parties. It should also be noted that in order to differentiate between various groups, some are unavoidably categorized which, in reality, might be less contradictory and more amorphous. It is sometimes artificial to divide them according to an ideological spectrum of right and left, when many of the differences are actually based on the personalities of the generals. With a perspective of several years, one can concede that there was initially a general tendency to exaggerate the

Table 8
Political Orientation of the Military Elite

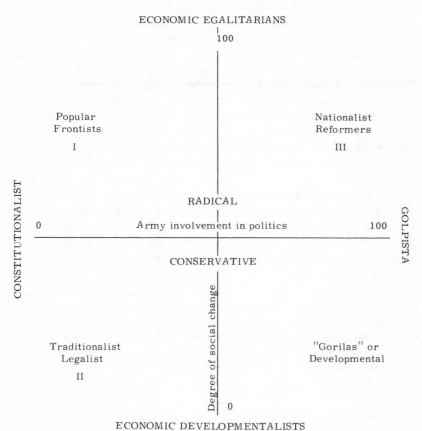

importance of ideological issues, rather than emphasize personality clashes and group rivalry as a major driving force.

Having stated this reservation as to the existence of clearcut classifications, it is nevertheless important to analyze how the different currents were perceived at the time of the crisis. For the sake of clarity, it is convenient to divide the decision-making elite into four categories, separated by two overlapping sets of coordinates: one from social change to conservatism, and the other from constitutionalist to interventionist. The first measures the degree of commitment towards the idea of narrowing the existing social gap and striving for a more egalitarian society. While in every case there is a strong emphasis on development, this is not always accompanied by the idea of limiting the wealth of the upper classes for the benefit of workers or peasants. The second coordinate reflects the difference between those officers who, though ready to influence the political procèss in a personal capacity, prefer to do it through the political party system, and those who prefer the direct involvement of the armed forces by taking upon themselves functions originally reserved for a democratically-elected government. This classification is represented in Table

The greater the military involvement in political life, the less the constitutionalist influence counted, and after February 1973, there were practically no declared constitutionalists left in the army decision-making elite. The personal composition of each of the four groups can be identified as follows:[9]

Popular Frontist: They identified with the Chilean experience. Among the outstanding personalities of this group was General Liber Seregni (ret.), presidential candidate of the Frente Amplio.[10] Also among the Frente Amplio supporters were Colonel Carlos Zufriatequi (ret.), General Victor Licandro (ret.), and General A. Balínez. General César Martínez (ret.), with a Colorado background, was dismissed as commander of the army in the February crisis; at the time of the *autogolpe*, Martínez proclaimed his adherence to the idea of a great civil front, "to the re-uniting of all Uruguayans in good faith,"[11] thereby receiving the support of the left.

Traditional Legalist: Its high-ranking officers adhered to the Blanco or Colorado parties, such as presidential candidates for the 1971 elections, General Juan P. Ribas (ret.) (a right-wing anti-Communist Colorado), and General Mario Aguerrondo (ret.) (Alianza Nacionalista, an "*acuerdista*" right-wing Blanco), at the very fringe between the "legalist" and "*gorila*" groupings. General Ventura F. Rodríguez discussed, together with Gral. César Martínez and Blanco W. Ferreira, the possibilities of preventing a military coup a few weeks before the *autogolpe*. General Francisco Gravina did not accept the army's becoming involved in the investigation of economic crimes and presented his resignation in the October 1972 crisis. Navy Captain Homar Murdoch (ret.) served as president of the National Directorate of the Partido Blanco[12] and was arrested for a short time along with other military men of the Frente Amplio after the *autogolpe*. General Antonio Francese (ret.) was unsuccessfully appointed by Bordaberry as minister of defense in the February crisis in order to counteract military pressure. In the navy, the influence of the Blanco's charismatic leader Wilson Ferreira Aldunate was great and resulted in the adoption of a general anticoup line, leading to the confrontation of February 1973 and the resignation of Rear Admiral Juan José Zorrilla.[13]

Nationalist Reformist: Considered as Peruvianists, they espoused the view that only through a progressive military regime could the country maintain intensive economic development, while changing the exploitative nature of the social structure and creating a foreign policy independent of the major dominating power, the United States. The best-known personality among them was General Gregorio Alvarez, who was in charge of the cojoint forces leading to the successful suppression of the Tupamaro movement. He was also the secretary of the powerful COSENA civil-military council, established after the February crisis. Others, though less defined, were General Eduardo Zubía, commander of the second military region,[14] and intelligence head Ramón Trabal. Captains Aguirregaray, Camacho, Rodríguez and Castro were also mentioned in October 1972 as initiators of a revolt at the Army Center that followed the Congress demands to punish officers that had been allegedly involved in the application of torture.[15]

"Gorilas" or Developmental: They leaned towards a pro-Brazilian stance, in spite of their denial of being influenced by foreign nations. With a more honest and efficent conduct of affairs, they would develop the country through unrestricted foreign investments. They were perhaps the most important element in the whole process, and included General Julio Vadora, chief of the third military region; the commander-in-chief of the army, General Hugo Chiappe Posse; and the commander of the first military region (Montevideo), General Esteban Cristi. All were known as "representatives of the extreme right."[16] Brigadier Pérez Caldas, chief of the air force, and Rear Admiral Víctor Gónzalez represented a more moderate tendency in the Gorila camp. The minister of the interior, Colonel Néstor Bolentini (ret.), who pursued the military's demands while inside the government, should also be included.

The formulation of the autogolpe consisted in presenting a unified stand by the army in the face of civilian institutions. It was rather difficult to achieve, due to the aforementioned internal discrepancies. It therefore required coalitions along one of the two axes on Table 8. While combinations I-IV or II-III were diametrically opposed, the others, I-II, I-III, III-IV, and II-IV, were possible. On a time sequence, while most I and II officers were left out of the army, the few that were still inside lost influence in the February crisis, during which III and IV presented a united front. As clear evidence of such a coalition, the leaders of both forces, Generals Gregorio Alvarez and Esteban Cristi, respectively, personally commanded the dissolution of the Parliament.[17]

From February 1973, the political position of the Peruvianists (III), whose political line had until then been reflected in the military's declarations, declined, while the Gorilas' power increased.[18] According to Sanguinetti:

> . . . if any line dominates the Uruguayan Army it is the conservative and authoritarian. They attempt, of course, to attract the people, and this pre-supposes demagogy, certain concessions to the masses, but no more.

It thereby means that for a long time there should not be expected any Peruvian deviation in the Uruguayan situation. If any model of development could serve as a source of inspiration to the actions of Bordaberry and the commanders, it is the Brazilian, in spite of the military's insistence on reiterating the uniqueness of their position.[19]

At the beginning of 1974, the Uruguayan regime adopted an even more pro-American foreign policy line than its immediate predecessors, with strong anti-Communist and anti-Soviet undertones. Internally, the traditional social structure was untouched and reforms were minimal, and the systematic persecution of the left provided further proof of the lack of a strong reformist tendency within the army leadership. Even if there were some ideological tension as to the rhythm of change and the distribution of wealth, the very fact that discrepancies on "secondary" policy issues were avoided brought about the postponement of new initiatives. Such a situation, in fact, strengthened those sectors which advocated immobilism and maintaining the status quo.

Thereby, what was considered to be a "developmental" position, later proved to be closer to the Chilean conservative sort of military regime, restrictive of any form of civilian organized political life. Curiously, in maintaining a civilian president as a figurehead, the long-run planning seems to aspire to creating a political structure resembling the present one in Brazil, with the two traditional parties functioning under strict control of the military, and the presidential candidate also under the close scrutiny of this corporate force.

COMMUNICATION

It is difficult to isolate the channels through which the operational environment was perceived by the military decision makers, and to then evaluate their impact upon their attitudinal prism. Although one can second-guess several paths, all lack explicit confirmation by the generals. In fact, the only path openly recognized as such by the military is the contact with the Tupamaros. Before elaborating this point, however, it is necessary to first provide some background information.

One of the main channels in Uruguay is the Instituto Militar de Estudios Superiores (IMES), which trains higher-ranking officers in military subjects, as well as "to facilitate the knowledge of the national reality and problems related to the national defense."[20] This is confirmed by Professor Armando Malet, for a brief time the defense minister preceding the February crisis. He revealed in an interview that one of the lectures that he delivered in the IMES a few months earlier was entitled, "The influence of the political parties' activities on the subversion process."[21] Most of the general conceptions of fighting against the urban guerrillas were developed in training provided by the United States, which also included political, psychological, and organizational aspects.[22]

Another possible source of influence on the military's attitude was the "Civic Action Program," launched with the assistance of the United States. In 1968, the army participated in several projects,[23] mainly in the poorer areas of the countryside, constructing bridges, roads, repairing classrooms, and so on. As was already mentioned, the importance of this was not only in the firsthand contacts with this type of reality, but in the effect it might have generated within the military regarding their determination to contribute to the development of their country. The program was probably instrumental in transmitting the values of "nation building."

Most of the military identified themselves with the traditional parties, whose newspapers were undoubtedly not only a source of information, but also later served as a source of criticism of their interventionist line. For the military elite, the mass media was important, as seen by their reaction to nearly all accusations, as in the case of Vasconcellos. This susceptibility is an indication of the media's impact on their perceptions, and perhaps a further reason for the imposition of total censorship on the press after the *autogolpe*.

One could also consider the extreme right-wing press as a means of strengthening the interventionist values. For example, an editorial in *Azul y Blanco* states:

> Enough with hypocrisy. Marxist and economic corruptors compose the groups of undesirable anti-nationals. And the Armed Forces know that well, even if they try with mermaid songs to confuse their course and send them into the abyss. Because of this, the Armed Forces made the great step forward; no more obstacles to the task of reconstructing the nation. ...Without personal ambitions and conscience of their transcendental mission, the generals of the Motherland, the honorable members of the Air Force and Navy, with a "military spirit," they gave the example of prudence, firmness and courage in a moment in which Uruguay seemed to be irremediably dying.[24]

In many cases, the commanders' contact with military and diplomatic foreign representatives encouraged their participation in political life; each new stage made them more important protagonists, and as such, a source of interest to foreign representatives.

However, what undoubtedly came to be accepted as the major channel motivating the military for political action was the face-to-face contact with the imprisoned Tupamaros.[25] "The presence of almost five thousand *Tupamaros* and activists of the marxist left confined in military dependencies made it inevitable that the dialogue between prisoners and jailors would produce a phenomenon of ideological transmission and the political conscience-raising of the military."[26]

The impact of the criticism against the government and the social situation was reinforced by a kind of admiration or respect that the army developed for the devotion and idealism of the Tupamaros and their readiness to die for their ideals. While the Tupamaros later dismissed the possibility that this direct contact produced a consciousness within the military elites, members of the army themselves admitted that they learned about reality in this way. In the antiinsurgency action, "each and all members of the Armed Forces met the national reality, a national reality that unavoidably leads to the destruction of our country if there is no immediate and energetic reaction on all levels."[27]

PSYCHOLOGICAL ENVIRONMENT: ATTITUDINAL PRISM AND ELITE IMAGES

The nearly total silence maintained by the various generals does not permit us to trace individual images and perceptions of the political entity. Even the collective expressions in the mass media are scarce and lack spontaneity. We are restricted, therefore, to mainly analyzing the texts of forty-six communiques issued by the "Junta de Comandantes" (the senior officers of the three army branches). This somewhat monotonous exercise gives us the declared position of the policy makers, although their actions do not always support their declared intentions. The advantage of such material is that it can be considered a culmination of the leaders' consensus. They are mostly technical announcements that were first delivered during the February crisis. As for the preceding period, unofficial documents, occasionally denied or rejected by the army officers as lacking validity, reflect internal trends of the different groups, exposing a lack of consensus on diverse issues. We shall briefly outline the major elements characterizing these documents.

Patriotism and Call of Duty

The patriotic role of the military in the decision to involve itself in national problems is stressed, for instance, in the declaration that, "The Army and Air Force, united in the patriotic duty of national reconstruction, maintain and will maintain at any moment a total ideological and material involvement for the benefit of the nation and the historic moment in which we all live."[28] "A moral duty, a committment towards the people," and so on.

Nationalism

The "nation building" values are upheld against group or class egoistic interests. "*Orientalidad*"[29] is the call for national effort, "as a consummation of the feelings of the population in the past, present and future, such that only with national solutions can Uruguayan men preserve their country from foreign influence, and whatever its orientation or origin, we shall find the way to prosperity, happiness and social justice."[30] All the sectors are called upon to join efforts for the common enterprise.

Superior Virtues

The civilian power lacks certain positive qualifications that are a natural attribute of the military. More specifically, "in the present state-controlled and public institutions, or what is even more grave in all fields, three essential virtues are not cultivated: discipline, a definite and clear sense of hierarchy and the cult of the personal and collective responsibility."[31]

Morality

The acts of corruption disclosed to the public emphasized the army's commitment to values such as integrity and honesty. Saving was proposed as a solution to reducing foreign debts (i.e., through drastically cutting trips abroad of Uruguayan diplomats or calling on the people, in a time of galloping inflation); the political parties were all regarded as infected by corruption.[32]

Efficiency

"The most capable people to the most suitable positions."[33] This slogan was offered when the military decided to involve their men in all public enterprises. "The integration of Armed Forces members in functions different from their specific objectives has to be based only on merit, on the recognition of their talents, and on moral qualities, responsibility, professional or technical capacity, united with a high spirit of personal sacrifice."[34]

Unity

During the February crisis, appeals to the navy to join the rebels were made, while stressing the instrumental value of army unity. "Technical capacity, unity of criteria, and popular support"[35] were considered the basis for political power.

Popular Origin

The fact was often emphasized that the people had to trust the army because they "never denied their popular origins."[36] "The Armed Forces are a genuine part of the Uruguayan people."[37]

Autonomy

"The Army is not the armed arm of any political and economic sector." It has already been mentioned that after overcoming the terrorist threat, the army wished to emphasize that they did not act in service of the regime and that they sought to continue their involvement in national problems, in opposition to the "illegal activities of government circles."[38]

Exclusive Philosophy

The Army's statements on political matters suggest that their position did not resemble ideologies of organized political groups. They maintained that those principles comprehensively represented a unique and original solution to the nation's problems. In any event, it is hard to conceive that a general consensus could have been reached among the generals on a given economic, social, and political problem; such a program was presented only once at a particular point of the process, probably due to both tactical and political reasons. This stage was represented in February 1973 Communiques Four and Seven, in which positions were adopted relating to several critical political and social problems. Afterwards, there was no further mention of radical political positions, only a reaffirmation of adherence to the principles in Communiques Four and Seven. The major principles adopted were: encouraging exports on an efficiency and quality basis; reorganizing the diplomatic service on a basis of personal capability and for the benefit of foreign trade; reducing expenditures in order to reduce the foreign debt; ending unemployment through public works and development projects; energetically persecuting illegal economic acts; reorganizing and rationalizing taxation and public administration; "redistributing" the land in order to give it to those who work it;[39] creating new occupational sources through the development of industry, according to national needs and practicability; appointing capable people to the direction of public enterprises; encouraging saving schemes; having the military participate in all institutions connected with defense and national security; struggling against monopolies and supporting workers' participation in the management of public and private enterprises; favoring credit for middle and small enterprises; encouraging the formation of cooperatives in the field of production; developing sources of energy; developing roads and means of transportation; modernizing; creating a technical level suitable for the needs of national development; having an income and pricing policy that will assure buying power at all levels without affecting production; having qualified medical assistance for all inhabitants; decentralizing; and building new enterprises and services in the rural areas.[40] Following disclosures of fraud and economic crimes, the army also insisted upon acquiring major control of the banking system in both the public and private sectors and certifying that it served the general interests of the nation.[41]

Interestingly, a somewhat vague formulation of the above principles was perceived in Uruguayan political circles as symbolizing the beginning of the radicalization of the military, thereby generating great hope, particularly among the left. Press coverage then often considered Communiques Four and Seven as "including ideas of a Marxist-cut type."[42] In one case, speculations went so far as to consider that the slogan "redistribution of land" would be implemented in a few months with the adoption of a land-reform law, and an "extraofficial" source of the army was even quoted as specifying the size of the latifundias that were to be expropriated.[43]

Consequently, it is extremely difficult to assess whether these political principles represented a growing consensus within the army about the respective topics concerning them, or rather an opportunistic scheme to capitalize upon popular sympathy, essential for further moves towards military intervention. In the long run, the abandonment of practically the entire program seems to indicate that the second answer may have been the correct one, since most of the Peruvianist generals continued to share power for quite a while and did not seem to be affected by the lack of commitment to the principles of Communiques Four and Seven.

On the other hand, negative images were mentioned during the course of this study, such as: anti-Marxism, anti-international Communism, opposition to politicization of trade unions, corruption, foreign interests, and "agent provocateurs." In addition, conditional support of the "democratic-republican" ideas existed, depending on the quality of the leadership: "From this point of view, we consider that our loyalty has to remain unchangeable towards the ruling principles of republican-democratic system of life, without mortgaging it in the hand of people, who with their personal ambitions or exaggerated egocentrism disregard the importance of personal sacrifice for the sake of the national welfare."[44] This paradoxical statement is rationalized in the acceptance of the civilian-military common enterprise in the "nation building" process.[45]

Again, it is difficult to provide a lucid picture as to how the military perceived the sundry internal and external constraints. The parsimonious expressions and self-restraint adopted by the military elite raise serious questions as to the utility of content analyzing the few sentences which, in many cases, were purposely evasive. As for the external setting, there is no evidence of perceived obstacles to the military's interventionist drive. On the contrary, it appears as if the decision makers themselves were encouraged by the attitude of the dominant superpower. One may appreciate their confidence in the support of the Nixon-Kissinger administration by recalling their deep disappointment and feelings of deception with the U.S. Congress' decision in 1976 to cut military aid to Uruguay. Frustration and anger were directed towards the Democrats, from which Senator Edward Kennedy was considered as the "best associate of subversion," and that he, for the sake of publicity, turned to help Castro and the Communists.[46] Anti-American sentiments became so widespread that an army journal had to reassure the "responsible officers" that such criticism was not aimed at the White House or the Pentagon, but at those in Congress, such as Edward Koch, who were instrumental in passing the ban on military aid.[47]

On the other hand, although the military generally associated Cuba with subversion in Latin America, no instances emerged of allegations of direct Castroist involvement in Uruguay, other than condemning Cuba's verbal support of the Frente Amplio in the 1971 elections as "intervention in internal affairs."

In fact, it is in the internal setting where the major obstacles were apparently perceived. Sharp reactions were vocalized towards two phenomena, subversion and corrupted parliamentarism, which in other words, meant that both the Tupamaros and Congress were seen as the principal enemies of the military. Criticism often linked these two forces, and in many cases, the military dealt with them separately.

It is unnecessary to elaborate at length the antagonism that the army developed towards the guerrillas. Condemning revolutionary violence, the navy officers declared war on "subversion which destroys the national economy, that frustrates the people from the fruit of his work, that propagates administrative, political or moral corruption, or that places in danger the national sovereignty [of Uruguay]."[48] Allegations of a possible truce with the Tupamaros were dismissed by the army in the strongest possible terms, claiming that "the Armed Forces have been dealing in no form whatsoever with criminal organizations which anti-patriotic goals are of general knowledge."[49]

The army attack on Congress is eloquently expressed in an exchange of incriminations with Senator Ferreira Aldunate. As to the allegations that the armed forces aimed at undermining the prestige of the civilian institutions, the Junta de Comandantes rebutted with a number of rhetorical questions:

a) Would it be economical to waste efforts to undermine the prestige of a Parliament already lacking prestige because of the corrupted practices which confront the highest national interests?

b) Who, if not the Parliamentarians, have vehemently defended the subversive movements, facilitating the publications of the statements of some of its Members (of Parliament) squashing the role played by the Armed Forces in the anti-subversive struggle and even blurring its action by appeals, requests of information, denunciations and criticism that did not seek anything else but to attenuate their own responsibility for the illnesses of the country; voting to grant legal attributions to the Armed Forces but that being conditional, deceitful and biased, it did not serve at all to ameliorate the operational capability of the forces.

Who allowed the destruction of the economy and the public morale, creating, furthering and defending the causes of the subversion, closing their eyes to the burdensome process of deterioration and corruption that affected the country over the last decades, sustaining a *depasse* and criminal liberalism?[50]

Although students and trade-union leaders were considered as members of the enemy's camp, they were not perceived as a serious threat. This assessment is corroborated in that it was only after finishing with the Tupamaros and Parliament that the military began suppressing these two leftist forces. The basic idea was to fight against the "ideological penetration of Marxist ideas, that reached alarming proportions inside the learning institutions and trade unions and a defeated sedition that was the consequence of these causes."[51]

The crucial element in the domestic structure, as perceived by the army, was the people, the "silent majority," not only unopposed to the growing military involvement, but favorably reacting to such a process. Their confidence was expressed in a secret document which expected the people to adopt an attitude of trust, namely, "If the military are doing it, it is because it is necessary."

According to Colonel Bolentini, the reasons for the public's support of the military can be captured in the following arguments: that the people are grateful to the armed forces because they put an end to governmental corruption; that the lack of respect by which they had been treated for years by the administration is going to change rapidly; that the promises made by political parties were difficult to implement, but now under the direction of the armed forces, such changes could be carried out effectively.[52]

DECISION-MAKING PROCESS:
IMPLEMENTATION AND FEEDBACK

In trying to pinpoint the precise time at which the army decided to execute the *autogolpe*, we encounter an unassailable obstacle of secrecy. We have elaborated in the appendix the major events unfolded during the analyzed period. On the basis of this sequence, it is difficult to discern to what extent the decisions resulted from compromises within the military elite or from a predetermined plan. However, it is known that clear tactical decisions were made in the successive crises leading to the strategic decision, that is, to assume absolute political power while keeping a nominal civilian president. The line was at one time defined as "adopting the political decisions that met the minimal resistance."[53]

From the beginning of the century until 1971, Uruguay was characterized by a low level of military intervention in politics. In the two cases of illegal acts by the executive—when President Terra dissolved the Congress in 1933, and when President Baldomir postponed elections in 1942—the armed forces did not participate, and it was the police and the fire brigade that controlled public order. It was only in September 1971, when the armed forces were brought in to lead the antisubversive action, that it gradually became involved in politics.

In the first crisis (October 1972), the possibility of resistance to the military moves existed, both for the president and the Congress. In both cases, however, the reaction was weak, a phenomenon which encouraged the military to proceed further. The February 1973 crisis, aimed at the executive, was used to consolidate the internal unity of the armed forces by forcing the navy to join. The president's surrender to the military's demands was accompanied by severe criticism from the liberals in Congress, who in turn, warned the army of the threat emanating from Parliament.

Consequently, the second strike was against Congress. The ultimatum was clear, when on March 23, the "Junta de Comandantes" warned that "this is the last appeal to wisdom and conciliation to the Parliament of the Republic," while "keeping the forces in a state of preparedness, to act at any moment in an orderly way in defense of the higher interest of the country and without prejudice of its normal duties."[54] The attack against Parliament contained charges of corruption and the demand for the suspension of parliamentarian immunity for Senator Erro. This last demand was transformed into a power struggle between the army and the Parliament, with the full understanding on both sides that acceptance of the army's demand would be a clear expression of surrender. With the failure of their ultimatum, the army implemented the *autogolpe* and dissolved both houses of the legislature. The only remaining barriers were the trade unions and the university. During the three crises, the army refused to intervene and interfere in the trade union/executive confrontation. Although stressing from time to time that the CNT should not involve itself in politics, it was only *after* the *autogolpe* that the army acted against the trade-union movement and the left at large.

In retrospect, everything seems to have been too well-planned for the army not to have met "unexpected" elements in its strategy. While admitting to such a possibility, it is quite clear that in dealing with its opponents one by one, they succeeded in dividing a possibly united civilian opposition. The question thus becomes, in what became the longest coup d'etat in history, whether the army elite planned from the very beginning of 1971 to take absolute power, or whether its appetite grew with its increasingly stronger political position. This writer believes that, until February 1973, the military leaders had not decided upon a policy and disagreed over the degree of involvement that was desirable, that is, whether at the level of public administration, ministerial, or absolute control. The view that the military involvement was more an incremental than a planned process is also suggested by McDonald: "The growth of the military participation was partially sequential, taking on different national institutions in a constantly escalating struggle.''[55]

The possibility did exist of maintaining a civil-military relationship with ''the military as orienters of national policy,''[56] but the middle way of intervention was fraught with dangers. A hostile Parliament was condemning them and the possibility of future opposition from the left-wing, and disenchanted sectors accelerated the decision to intervene and become the ''dictators behind the President.'' It therefore seems that the strategic decision to follow one of the two alternatives: *autogolpe* (the most realistic one), or the surrender of parliamentarian independence to the army, was taken only after the army's political success in the February crisis. The grave accusations against the congressmen that followed in March were clearcut evidence that such a line was adopted. The obstinacy of the congressmen in refusing total surrender gave way to the fulfilment of the second alternative. While the general trend in the army since 1971 was to involve itself in politics, the final extent and degree was determined only in the course of the process itself.

It is worthwhile to introduce some brief remarks concerning the distinction between *strategic* and *tactic* decisions. In the case of the military takeover in Uruguay, the dissolution of Congress on June 27, 1973 is generally regarded as making the transition from a civilian to a military regime. If one adopts this line of argument, it is possible to single out the first weeks of May 1973, in which the practical preparation apparently began to be mounted for the possible coup a month later.[57] It could then be technically possible to refer to a strategic decision's taking place at this particular date. However, the incremental nature of the military involvement in Uruguay over a long period of time instead pinpoints the two crises preceding the *autogolpe*, October 1972 and February 1973, as having been as decisive to the outcome as the last one. It is therefore important to separately consider the three major confrontations, for each required a major decision from the military decision makers. Therefore, as it becomes somewhat artificial to differentiate in this particular case study between the two levels of decisions, it is necessary to regard the process as a continuum, in which certain resolutions were more salient than others.

The effect of the feedback element on the decision of the military elite undoubtedly played a crucial role. The relatively slow escalation in the process of their political involvement gave ample opportunity at each of the stages to check the reactions of the other political components. Most likely, the military sensed an encouraging apathy from the external environment. In the internal environment, the rapid surrender of the executive, the lack of coordination in time and the conflict between the traditional and reformist forces in Parliament, and a perceived tacit acquiescence from the general population might have influenced the decision to proceed to absolute power. The possible absence of a preplanned strategic decision confirms the importance of feedback on the psychological environment of the decision makers.

NOTES

1. According to the *Area Handbook*, the total number of the armed forces for 1970 was 17,000, equal to the number in the maritime and national police. These last two forces were traditionally run by a general or rear admiral. Thomas E. Weil, et al., *Area Handbook for Uruguay* (Washington: American University, 1971), p. 383.

2. Argentina's army strength for 1967 is estimated at 132,000 men and Brazil's at 194,350, compared to Uruguay's 17,000. David Wood, *Armed Forces in Central and South America* (London: Adelphi Papers, 1967), pp. 21–23.

3. *Keesing's Contemporary Archives*, 25690, January 22–28, 1973. Apparently referring to *army* generals only.

4. Weil, p. 392. Three brigadier generals in the air forces, four rear admirals in the navy, and fourteen generals in the army. The number of colonels is estimated at 195.

5. Gabriel Ramírez, *Las Fuerzas Armadas Uruguayas en la Crisis Continental* (Montevideo: Tierra Nueva, 1971), p. 198. In the case of the navy, it is usually considered that the majority of the junior officers will come from a higher class, either with a good economic position, or simply as sons of military officers. The political tendency there is more conservative and constitutionalist.

6. *La Opinión*, August 16, 1974.

7. See section dealing with the competing elites in chapter 3.

8. *La Opinión*, October 24, 1972.

9. Surely, some personal views have been changed during the process, and the actual identification of their ideas is even more difficult, since most of the information is based on rumors and secondary sources.

10. His early retirement at the end of 1968 was caused by his dissatisfaction with the growing use of the armed forces in repressive acts against popular sectors, the compulsory mobilization of strikers, etc. Considered during his army service as a Colorado with left leanings, his departure was accompanied by a letter of support published by an unidentified group of young officers in the daily *Extra* on November 9, 1968. See Ramírez, pp. 281–300.

11. While stressing the need of change and unity among Uruguayans at this very critical moment, General Martinez, even if critical of the present functioning of the political parties, admitted that "I must point out, as a matter of principle, that I do not conceive of any country without political parties. It is therefore an aspiration and a desire that should embrace every body that these parties will rapidly find the way of the mentioned re-structuration," *Ultima Hora*, June 27, 1973.

12. *La Opinión*, July 25, 1973. Navy Captains Bernardo Pynerua (president of the Navy Club) and H. Camps were arrested for thirty days for defending Captain Murdoch. The military judge considered their declaration of his innocence to constitute disrespect of the authorities.

13. Zorrilla stated that he did not disagree with the objectives of the rebels, but only with their method. *Jerusalem Post*, February 12, 1973.

14. From all four military regions, number 1 is the smallest in geographic terms but the strongest in quantitative terms because of its proximity to the nerve centers of the country. Number 2 is considered the second in importance.

15. *La Opinión*, June 28, 1973.

16. Article of Richard Gott, in *The Guardian*, London, March 22, 1973. Opinions differ about Chiappe Posse, some considering him more in the middle between developmental and traditional legalists.

17. *El País*, June 29, 1973.

18. Carlos López Matteo, "The Process Seems to Characterize Itself by A Suppressive Turn to the Right." *La Opinión*, May 15, 1973.

19. Ibid., July 18, 1973.

20. See brochure of IMES, Montevideo, Uruguay, undated. The general impression is that the "ideological" side of the studies is much less pronounced than in the Peruvian CAEM, which provided the radical leadership for the national reformist military regime in this country. According to Gabriel Ramírez, it is incorrect to think that the young officers are radicals. On the contrary, their separation from society at an early age and their background make them regularly more conservative than the superior officers, who through promotion courses in IMES have acquired a wider knowledge of the national reality (Ramírez, p. 208). He finds evidence in the *Cuadernos* published by IMES.

21. *Marcha*, February 23, 1973.

22. Ramírez, see chapter dealing with "training and introduction," pp. 137–52; and *NACLA*, 10 (1976): 21–23, outline of course on "Urban Counter-Insurgency Operations."

23. Weil, p. 393.

24. Secret document mentioned in October by Defense Minister Legniani, in A. Vasconcellos, *Febrero Amargo* (Montevideo), p. 116. According to General César Martínez (ret.), "the military, in the anti-subversive struggle, had learned terms of the political equation that before were not taken into consideration. They came to know antagonistic interests, the political leadership of the States, and all of the situation where they lived," *El Día*, June 26, 1973.

25. *Azul y Blanco*, February 14, 1973.

26. *La Opinión*, June 17, 1973.

27. Héctor Gutiérrez Ruiz, "Las Fuerzas Armadas y la Realidad del País," *Estrategia* (Buenos Aires) 19–20 (1972–73): 17–30.

28. *Cuadernos de Marcha*, February 23, 1973, p. 25.

29. "Orientalidad" comes from the official name of the country, República Oriental del Uruguay, and has the meaning of nationalism or patriotism.

30. *El País*, July 4, 1973.

31. Interview with minister of interior, Colonel Néstor Bolentini, *Marcha*, February 23, 1973.

32. See communique of the "Junta de Comandantes" on January 19, 1973, calling on the president to take action against the irregularities in the Departmental City Council of Montevideo, *Marcha*, February 2, 1973; and interview with former minister of defense, A. Malet, *Marcha*, February 23, 1973, p. 10.

33. *La Opinión*, April 5, 1973.

34. *Cuadernos de Marcha*, February 23, 1973, p. 15.

35. Vasconcellos, p. 119.

36. *Cuadernos de Marcha*, p. 20.

37. *La Opinión*, July 8, 1973. "A dual purpose social movement has to be produced: from the people to the Armed Forces and from the Armed Forces to the people. The result of the first will be that, better than ever, the Armed Forces will receive the impulse of the spirit of the nation; through the second, it will be possible to orient the citizens in the ways of order, discipline, responsibility and productive and well distributed work." Interview with Colonel Bolentini, *Marcha*, May 14, 1973.

38. *La Opinión*, March 9, 1973.

39. It is important to stress this fundamental difference from the left, who openly spoke of "agrarian reform" and not "the land to those who work it," which could be landowners as well as peasants.

40. *Cuadernos de Marcha*, pp. 23–25, 31–34. (army communiques number four and seven, February 1973. Afterwards there was no further mention of reduced political positions, but only a general reaffirmation of adherence to the mentioned documents.)

41. *La Mañana*, October 12, 1972.

42. *Clarín*, February 11, 1973.

43. *La Opinión*, March 14, 1973.

44. *El País*, February 10, 1973.

45. This lip service paid to civilians is shown through conserving the elected president. Thus the army could continue to speak, even after the *autogolpe*, of "supporting the government," or stating that "obviously the civil authorities continue to stand at the head of the country, and the Armed Forces merely contribute to consolidating and backing them," *La Opinión*, July 8, 1973.

46. *Grisur, Grupo de Información y Solidaridad Uruguay*, 57 (1976): 1. Quoting *La Mañana*, October 9, 1976.

47. Centro Militar, *El Soldado*, October 9, 1976.

48. *Le Monde*, March 20, 1973.

49. *Clarín*, August 2, 1972.

50. Declaration of the Junta de Comandantes, May 13, 1973; *Mancha*, May 16, 1973.

51. *La Opinión*, December 8, 1972.

52. *Marcha*, May 14, 1973.

53. Vasconcellos, p. 101. It could also be argued that it was mainly due to the weakness of the political forces in the internal setting, rather than the calculated risks taken by the army leaders, that produced the rapid collapse of the civil institutions.

54. *Marcha*, June 30, 1973.

55. Ronald H. McDonald, "The Rise of Military Politics in Uruguay," *Interamerican Economic Affairs* 28 (1975): 26.

56. Gino Germani and Kalman Silvert, "Politics, Social Structure and Military Intervention in Latin America," in *Government and Politics in Latin America*, ed. Peter G. Snow (New York: Holt, Rinehart & Winston, 1967), p. 315.

57. *Clarín*, May 21, 1973. An officer of the Uruguayan army disclosed that a few days earlier, it was decided to suppress the representative institutions in June. At the same time, he argued that there were still internal obstacles to overcome, regarding the objections of elements in the navy to a military takeover.

5.
The Post-Crisis Stage:
The Military in Power

DECISION-MAKING ELITE

More than four years after the *autogolpe*, the military's involvement in Uruguay seems to have stabilized, for all practical purposes representing a total takeover, while simultaneously insisting on showing a certain loyalty towards the "legal" institutions. Shortly before the end of Bordaberry's term of office, the military had to consider the question of whether he should be allowed to remain in office for a further unspecified period, some type of formula for the nomination of another candidate should be devised, or a military junta should be established. Bordaberry's own proposal, in a widely-published "secret memorandum" of December 1975 and June 1976, showed his preference for "constitutional reforms to set up an absolute, corporativist state with an all-powerful executive and legislative body composed of representatives from the landowners, industrialists, and professionals. The political parties would be dissolved to prevent their being used as Marxist fronts." [1] This self-postulation was used on June 12 by the military as the very excuse to forcibly remove him, arguing that the functioning of the traditional political parties and the practice of universal suffrage be ultimately reestablished. [2]

On July 14, Dr. Aparicio Méndez, a 71-year-old lawyer, was appointed by the Council of the Nation (composed of 25 civil members of the Council of State and 21 military members of the Junta of Generals) as president of Uruguay. His appointment was formally proposed by the head of the armed forces, General Julio César Vadora, and in the voting that followed, only two members of the electing council opposed his nomination.

73

The selection of Méndez as the new president did not come as any surprise and had been widely predicted several days before the voting took place. Since June, Aparicio Méndez (71 years old when elected) had acted as the president of the Consejo de Estado, replacing Alberto Demichelli (80 years old), who at that time was appointed as interim president for a period of two months. Méndez was therefore the next obvious candidate in the line of succession to the presidency.

It is not expected that the appointment of Méndez as president will bring about any major changes in the situation in Uruguay. When his appointment was announced, Méndez was the first to point out that he owed his position to the trust and collaboration of the armed forces. He also gave assurances to the press that the process of "national recuperation" would continue in Uruguay "without changes, modifications or reformulations."

Facing growing constraints, the reaction of the military over time has been to intensify repression and increasingly monopolize total power. Its decision to force Bordaberry's resignation and their formal involvement in the appointment of the new president is but one expression of such a process. Following the elimination of the legislative power in June 1973, the authority of the heads of the military districts on the local level has become the commanding force. While in practice the process of justice was long ago paralyzed by the use of military tribunals, the independence and attributions of the judiciary power were finally curtailed by the Institutional Act No. 8 in July 1977, by which the executive can freely appoint, remove, or dismiss members of the High Court of Justice, since the judges' rulings were considered "insufficient and inefficient facing the present reality." [3]

At the same time, the ruling elite has found its civilian and military basis of support steadily eroding. As the removal of elected president Bordaberry severed the last civilian legitimation to the regime, it was thus expected that the military would endeavor to find a respectable civilian figure who, although appointed and not elected by popular vote, could command some respect on his own merits. The two best known contenders for the presidency were former Economy Minister Alejandro Vegh Villegas and Foreign Minister Carlos Blanco. The former, apparently backed by the U.S. embassy in Montevideo, did not concede to the military's pressure to appoint their men to high-ranking jobs in the Ministry of Economy and insisted on trimming the enormous military expenditures in the national budget, accounting for 52 percent of its total. [4] Blanco, on the other hand, clearly aware of the negative repercussions that Uruguay's violations of human rights have had in the capitals of the West and particularly the United States, hesitated to keep his post under Méndez. When the president undiplomatically referred to the U.S. Democratic party as "communist inspired," Blanco's energetic criticism helped the military to rectify the president's statement but simultaneously facilitated the acceptance of his resignation as foreign minister.

The generals, therefore, preferred Méndez's willingness to passively submit to the armed forces rather than the other two candidates' threatening claims for greater freedom of action. In substance though, the military has pledged to adhere to a transitional scheme towards civilian rule, designed by Villegas and following, to a great extent, the Brazilian model. According to this plan for a limited return to democratic rule, Aparicio Méndez will remain in office for five years. He will then be replaced by a common candidate chosen by the two traditional parties with the approval of the military. Elections with two candidates, again from the traditional parties and approved by the military, have been announced to be scheduled for about 1986.

There is still, however, no official guarantee that this proposed return to a restricted democracy will ever take place. Even if it is realized, this proposed solution has been categorically rejected by all the political parties, from the traditional Blanco to the illegal Communist one.

The growing inner weakness of the military elite as a corporative body is of even greater significance. Many coups have been characterized by the prominent role played by a single general, such as Chile's General Pinochet. Uruguay's generals, however, failed to find within their midst a dominating personality who could take the lead.[5] One explanation for the continuation of the civilian presidency is precisely this absence of inner agreement among the military as to who amongst them could become a *primus inter pares*. In fact, it was even difficult for the generals to reach a consensus as to the basic idea of executing the *autogolpe*. As was mentioned in the preceding chapter, the top navy leadership was removed, other generals dismissed, and some even arrested. However, dissent was not eliminated; on the contrary, personal involvement in repressive activities has generated among certain elements feelings of dismay and disapproval. International uproar resulted from a letter from an anonymous "patriotic" Uruguayan officer, who in February 1976 addressed a letter to the Vatican confessing his repudiation of the acts of torture he had witnessed and even participated in. He sent accompanying shocking photographs of such cases.[6]

At the beginning of 1977, a nucleus of between twenty and fifty officers were arrested, tortured, and sentenced to imprisonment when a document, drafted prior to the *autogolpe*, was discovered. The document—in which the signatures were chosen by lottery, that is, only one out of a set number of officers signing and exposing himself—discussed the possibility of preempting the incumbent coup. However, they were not able to carry it out, and over three years later the document was discovered. Many of these responsible are sons of high-ranking officers, and among them colonels.

Furthermore, on March 26, 1977, a reliable report was published about a secret meeting of commanders in the Fortress of Santa Teresa. It lasted fifteen hours, at which time criticism was directed at the policies of the military in government and a call for a "positive and beneficial outcome" was sounded.[7]

Apparently, a similar demand for a quick return to democracy was also previously voiced by a group of officers during 1976. In any event, the Uruguayan regime had great difficulties in denying the many reports of dissent among its ranks and the arrest of the authors of such a memorandum.[8]

Another account in mid-April 1977 mentions a plenary meeting of colonels of the different branches who, although reaffirming their support for their superiors, nevertheless demanded modifications of policies and ministerial figures, as well as the acquittal of the authors of the March memorandum, which in their opinion emanated from none other than patriotic considerations and due respect to authority and rank.[9]

Special legislation was introduced in order to purge from the armed forces those officers apt to challenge the official line. On April 21, 1977, an amendment to the Organic Military Law was approved, by which any officer could be obliged to retire by a decision of four-fifths of the members of the Junta of Generals of the respective branches (or by unanimity if less than five participate in the decision). This was not a theoretical exercise, but a measure that was quickly implemented. Already in May 1977, it was reported that enforced retirement was applied to forty rear admirals and navy captains, which left only about half of the original number in active duty.[10]

All these elements are important for understanding the difficulties presented in ensuring continuity in a corporative regime in which the upper ranks are supposed to give room to their subordinates in a traditionally rapid turnover. Many of the originators of the *autogolpe* have already retired, and in 1977, an attempt to extend for one year the office of two leading figures, representing two different camps, was undermined by the resignation of one of them (General Eduardo Zubía). He was welcomed since it precipitated the withdrawal of the other (the hardliner General Esteban Cristi). As for those founders of the *autogolpe* remaining among the elite, personal recriminations and rivalry are also hampering any consolidated effort. The promotion of the personalistic and former Peruvianist, Colonel Gregorio Alvarez could possibly be prevented by maintaining the rather uncontroversial General Vadora as commander in chief. The problem of the chain of command is well summarized in the words of a civilian figure of the Uruguayan government: "The younger officers are exerting excessive pressure asking that the 'old ones' (meaning the generals) and the 'mature ones' (meaning the colonels) be put into retirement and at the same time that the country be directed along the path of legality which it should never have abandoned."[11]

It is doubtful whether the long-term controlled political outcome of Vegh Villegas will be pursued. More immediate solutions have been informally contemplated, such as seeking the more respected general to fulfill the role of pacifier, who will assure a fast but orderly transition to civilian rule. Or, alternatively, and perhaps more suitable for the complex civilian-military faction in Uruguay, will be the dismissal of Méndez and his replacement by a civilian-military junta which would include leading and respectable independent politicians.[12]

INTERNAL SETTING

No real threat to the military's power can be traced as emanating from the domestic structure. As Uruguay is a country with a strong democratic tradition, potential large foci of opposition have been silenced with a high level of repression. The legal system itself has become a most restrictive set of rules. Guarantees of individual rights have been suspended, and since such an authority which resided in the Congress was dissolved by the executive in June 1973, no safeguards whatsoever remain. Not only have basic rights been eliminated (opinion, assembly, speech, etc.), but various new limitations have been added, such as the obligation of all public servants, including teachers, to take the "oath of democratic faith" to demonstrate that they have never belonged to any organization which has attacked the existing system of government. Much of the punitive legislation is applied retroactively to civilians by military jurisdictions, such as membership in political organizations considered to be of a "subversive character" (penalty three to eighteen years) or "attacking the morale of the Army and Navy" (penalty sixteen months to 6 years). One of the most extreme cases of flagrant repressive legislation is the law of the "State of Dangerousness." [13] The law penalizes the *"inclination to commit crimes"* and provides for up to six years confinement with labor though *"no offence has been committed."* The law gives a cloak of legality to the existing malpractices and can, with its vague wording, apply to nearly every Uruguayan citizen "a sword of Damocles" to silence all opposition. A member of the Council of State was recently quoted in a Uruguayan newspaper as saying that it will preempt international criticism regarding the large number of persons in detention without a formal judicial warrant. As the council is designated by the executive power, the bill is expected to be passed without much delay.

The most sinister nature of the law is related, however, to the present political reality of Uruguay and to other legislation already in force, such as the Law of National Security and the Military Penal Code. To an increasing extent, people are being tried under charges such as "attack on the morale of the Armed Forces" which in fact means any criticism of the policies of the present de facto regime. Nor is it possible, with a muzzled press, and with no parliament or political parties, for the citizen to discuss what the "national values" are, or what is intended by "disturbing the effective development of preventive or executive action taken by the state to combat subversion." After a recent public accusation of defense lawyers by the armed forces that they share the ideology of their clients and are at the service of subversive elements, lawyer contacts have expressed the fear that their presentation of a legal defense will be classified under the above heading.

A defense lawyer, Mario Dell'Acqua, has in fact recently been arrested and charged with "assistance to subversive association," and the "incriminating evidence" quoted by the prosecutor includes his defense of twenty-five political prisoners. Also, recent charges against prisoners have cited their collecting monies for material relief to families of political prisoners.

Various sections of the proposed new law related directly to the "ideology of violence," notably Marxism. Consequently, being a Marxist, having Marxist friends, or having Marxist books would cause a person to fall under this law. So would spreading information "in or outside the country" on torture and other abuses of authority.

The text itself and these comments will suffice to show that the law of the "State of Dangerousness" can be applied to nearly every Uruguayan citizen and is, with its vague wording, an obvious attempt to silence all opposition and prevent help to political prisoners and their families, while at the same time attempting to preempt international criticism by giving the repression a cloak of legality.

The court procedure in the military tribunals does not give much hope for a fair trial. Persons suspected of terrorism, subversion, or other crimes against the nation are subject to the Internal Security Laws and decrees which suspend Article 15 (inviolability of the person from arrest except on probable cause), Article 16 (the right of the arrested person to be brought before a judge within twenty-four hours in the presence of his attorney), and Article 17 (habeas corpus). There is no discernible pattern as to the length of time persons are detained without being charged and tried. Most who are detained are eventually charged with specific crimes under the Law of State Security and Internal Order and the Military Penal Code. Actual trial is often considerably delayed. The 200 or so political prisoners being held at "the disposition of the Executive" are held without charges. Defense lawyers are not permitted access to their clients in pretrial proceedings; however, they are permitted access in later stages of judicial proceedings. The prohibition against lawyers during the stage of pretrial investigations is crucial because persons charged with subversion are often held incommunicado for long periods of time. This problem is compounded at later stages of the judicial process by the fact that the role of lawyers in defending alleged subversives may be inhibited, since proceedings take place in a military court system manned by military judges not trained in the law and reportedly often hostile to civilian lawyers.

The implementation of the repressive legislation is carried out to its fullest expression, and practices are often even more extreme than the written text. A preliminary comment should be made about the scope of political imprisonment in Uruguay. In its 1975 annual report, Amnesty International assessed the number of prisoners at approximately 5,000, which means that one in every 500 citizens has been under political detention, and an average of one in every 50 citizens has suffered interrogation or short-term detention in recent years. Uruguay, therefore, has the highest per capita ratio of political prisoners in Latin America.[14]

Torture, however, has been the most salient feature of human rights violations in Uruguay, which in the words of Senator Frank Church is "the biggest torture chamber in Latin America."[15] The instruments are most varied and include long lists of physical methods (electric prod, "submarine," "dry submarine," *plantón*, "sawhorse," "banner," "grill," tying the prisoner to a horse or vehicle, etc.) and psychological methods (simulated executions, permanent blindfolds, threats to family members, etc.).[16]

The brutality in which these methods are used can be documented by Amnesty International's record of approximately forty cases of death under torture, supported by reports from many independent observers and a large number of testimonies.

Political persecution is not confined merely to the borders of Uruguay itself but also extends to its neighboring states, particularly to Argentina, where a large colony of political exiles settled after the *autogolpe*. Among the most spectacular was the kidnapping and killing of four Uruguayans in May 1976, and among them, two leading opposition figures, Senator Zelmar Michelini of the Frente Amplio, and the chairman of the House of Deputies, Congressman Héctor Gutiérrez Ruiz.

Many young Uruguayans disappeared in Buenos Aires. A substantial number of them were alleged members or sympathizers of the Resistencia Obrera Estudiantil (Workers-Students Resistance, ROE), and some of their bodies were later found on the Uruguayan coast of the Plate River or in jails in Montevideo. The widely publicized case of the kidnapping in Buenos Aires and subsequent release in Montevideo of the prominent journalist, Enrique Rodríguez Larreta[17] does not leave much room for further doubts about the close cooperation between the Uruguayan and Argentinian secret services.

Such being the general picture, it thus explains the reasons for the suppression of all types of violent opposition, and peaceful dissent being expressed in a most cautious form.

Although the functioning of the traditional parties has been banned, informal meetings sporadically crop up. Colorado member Jorge Batlle apparently made public his criticism of the military regime, feeling somewhat protected by the growing interest of the U.S. administration in the human rights situation in Uruguay.[18] The Blanco party heavily centers around its major leader, Senator Ferreira Aldunate, who, exiled in London, maintains an efficient clandestine communications network. A basic agreement "to struggle to overthrow the dictatorship" was seemingly worked out between the Blancos and Colorados at the end of 1976. With some of their members in prison, as well as in the case of the Christian Democratic party, traditional opposition inside the country does not reflect organized activities. The Communists have also suffered heavily from repression. Although belonging to the leftist camp that never approved of the use of violence for social change, they have, following the destruction of the Tupamaros, become a target of repression. After banning them in December 1973, the regime at first arrested only the major national leaders, but by October 1975 launched a raid of huge dimensions, arresting between 700 and 1,000 members[19] and thereby completely dismantling the middle-level cadres. Other militants have been encouraged to leave Uruguay, first to Argentina, and after the military coup of March 1976, to other countries. It is hard to assess the size of the clandestine Communist network remaining in Uruguay, for barring the distribution of bulletins and the painting of slogans around May 1, little is known about their activity.

The leaders of the Communist-led and once powerful trade union movement (CNT) are either in jail or exile. Since March 1974, all trade union activities have been prohibited. Strikes are not tolerated. Even elections of new boards have been paralyzed and workers meetings on trade union matters (salaries, etc.) have been banned; in the few cases where such meetings have taken place, participants have been arrested, and many are still in detention without trial. Although the CNT has been totally restricted from any attempt to register political opposition to the regime, trade union activities per se are perceived by the government as a threat. Due to the increasing gap between prices and salaries, the workers' discontent continues to be shown on many occasions, and such expressions are also severely repressed.

Trade union premises have been taken over by the authorities, and in the outstanding case of the Building Workers' Trade Union, their headquarters were transformed by the authorities into a torture chamber. "A special fund was created in Uruguay for the building of houses with a 2% deduction from the wages of all workers in Uruguay .... The houses were never built, the funds being used to pay the wages of the army and police."[20]

The International Labor Organization (ILO) rejected a government-controlled trade union's (Confederacion General de Trabajadores del Uruguay, CGTU) bid to gain international recognition. It continued instead to recognize CNT as the workers' representative and published reports in November 1976 and May 1977 which underlined serious restrictions on trade union freedom in Uruguay.

The university and high school network has become completely neutralized as a political force, deprived of its traditionally independent character. Teachers (regular or specialized), school principals, inspectors, and technical supervisors for the public school system had always been appointed by merit through scholastic competition (known as "*oposiciones*"). Under the "Education Law," high-ranking positions in the school system (e.g., that of principal) became "positions of confidence"—that is, appointments were no longer made through scholastic competition; instead, the Uruguayan authorities named to these positions individuals deemed to be "friendly to the regime."

Now, according to Decree No. 28, a teacher not only has to make the already mentioned statement of support to the regime, but must prove that he does not belong to any organization which "aims at destroying the principles of the nationality" and he must repudiate regimes that "according to their ideology, pursue these aims." [21] By applying their laws, and also by going far beyond the limits of their own legality, the authorities have virtually destroyed the public school system; they have dismissed, for political reasons, without guarantees or legal procedures, hundreds of principals, inspectors, and teachers who had dedicated years and years of their work and whose personal and professional records were impeccable. (This is clear, since not one of these individuals has been dismissed for professional reasons or even accused of failing to meet professional standards).

What was originally an attempt to depoliticize the university facilitated the introduction of a new "philosophy," whose reactionary character is well described by Professor Martin Weinstein, taking as his example the curriculum of the course "Sociology of Education." [22]

The activities of other pressure groups also have little impact on Uruguayan politics. The church, which initially was cast to play the role of the only accepted opposition group, decided after personally receiving threats to considerably lower its profile.

Paradoxically, the weakest of all political pressure groups in the country—with 368 working groups (*grupos de reflexión*)—constitutes an institution to which it is very difficult to apply the normal restrictions. Conscious of their unique role, the Catholic church prelates have tried to use the church as a means of mass communication to stress the public condemnation of the flagrant violations of human rights in Uruguay. A recent example was the pastoral letter, signed by the fifteen bishops of the Uruguayan Episcopal Conference, which was to be read in all churches on October 12, 1975. The text included an appeal for "the widest possible amnesty" and a "withdrawal from the philosophy of hatred and violence." At the last moment, the government banned its publication and the church withdrew the letter from circulation to parishes and media.

The former auxiliary bishop of Montevideo, Andrés Rubio, summed up the situation as follows: "The Uruguayan police tentatively watches the Catholic Church, controls and watches the content of the sermons in the churches and investigates the text of the material circulated; several parishes and houses of clergymen have been subjected to searches and some priests have been arrested." [23]

The regime has also encountered diminished support in the countryside. Many of the members of the Board of the Rural Federation are openly antagonistic to the regime, and the former secretary of this organization, Ing. Horacio Terra Gallinal, was imprisoned several times because of his militant stand in the Blanco party. The landowners[24] also have criticized the regime's economic policy, but this hostility was curbed by the military's appointing a banker who does not possess any land as the new president of the federation.

The press continues to be severely restricted. According to the U.S. State Department's field report on human rights in Uruguay, "direct media criticism of the government is almost non-existent and espousal of Marxist and extremist philosophies is not tolerated. The media operates under a system of self-censorship within guidelines established by the authorities".[25]

It is important to explain that there is, in fact no opposition press. With the closure of the Blanco newspaper, *El Civismo*, in the city of Rocha, all media is manipulated by the regime. What accounts for differences of opinions among the newspapers in many ways may represent the different tendencies inside the military establishment. For instance, in the case of a famous speech of President Méndez, *El Día*—generally unwilling to praise the regime—severely criticized his speech,[26] while the more docile *La Mañana* reacted favorably.[27] In any event, the authorities may decide in advance to eliminate references to a certain issue (i.e., instructions forbidding any mention of the speech of the American delegate to the eighth meeting of the Interamerican Council for Education, Science and Culture (CIECC) that met in Montevideo in February, 1977),[28] or alternatively and post factum, to confiscate the entire edition of the newspaper.

The deterioration of the standard of living, the continuous meat ban, inflation, and massive exodus are surely not sparking additional popularity for the government among large sectors of the population. It is difficult to interpret whether the passivity of the people has a rather negative connotation or if it represents an attitude of approval of the authorities. The regime has tried to prove the latter by showing that 48 percent of the Uruguayans believe that human rights are respected in Uruguay (17 percent to a certain extent and 7 percent not at all)[29] and by Méndez's referring to only a third of the Uruguayans being associated with subversion, thus being enemies of the regime.[30]

EXTERNAL SETTING

The influence of the external setting on political processes in Uruguay has varied over time. The Uruguayan regime consolidated its position concurrently with the Southern Cone's transformation into a rather homogeneous military ruled area. Although such a development helped strengthen the position of the government in Montevideo, it has dramatically fallen into increasing isolation on the international level, encountering particular ostracization from the West.

While political opposition inside Uruguay has become nearly untenable, the large number of exiles, many with vast political experience, have been quite instrumental in arousing international public opinion about repression in their respective countries. Furthermore, voluntary international organizations, such as Amnesty International and the International Commission of Jurists, have attached considerable importance to the struggle for the respect of human rights in Uruguay, a subject that has strongly influenced the policy of many European governments and the United States.

As aforementioned, Uruguay has found its major allies in the Latin American subsystem to lie in the south. Bordaberry's visit to Bolivia and Chile, Paraguayan President Stroessner's and Argentinian General Videla's journeys to Uruguay, and President Méndez's trip to Brazil clearly depict the web that has been forged between these military regimes. Collaboration in the repression of opposition circles in exile[31] is now being corroborated by their common stand against President Carter's new policy of linking cuts in military aid to those recipient countries demonstrating a pattern of gross violations of human rights. Uruguay's relationship with Brazil has the added dimension of a strong dependence on its powerful neighbor's economic policy. Importing 28 percent of its total foreign trade from Brazil (U.S. $162 million) and exporting only half of this amount, the negative balance of payments is growing.[32]

The idea of close military cooperation between the armies of the Southern Cone of Latin American has been expanded by the head of the navy, Rear Admiral Hugo Márquez, who suggested a South Atlantic Military Treaty Organization to include South Africa and to be supervised by the United States.[33]

It is in the more northern part of the continent that the Uruguayan regime has met with difficulties. Venezuela, itself under civil rule, has been boldly outspoken in its criticism. In 1975, the Venezuelan Senate adopted a resolution which in very clear terms "condemns as contrary to the noble democratic tradition of the Uruguayan nation and the vocation of liberty of the whole American community, and as spurious in origin, the oppressive and unpopular regime now tyrannizing our sister country."[34] A few months later, the Venezuelans severed diplomatic relations with Uruguay. This followed an incident in which the Uruguayan police violated the extraterritorial rights of the Venezuelan Embassy in Montevideo by forcefully abducting a woman who was trying to gain political asylum. This was the first case of a country's interrupting diplomatic relations with Uruguay and symbolically resembled Mexico's severance of relations with the military junta in Chile. Since then, Venezuela has not hesitated to support any motion furthering human rights in Uruguay, especially within the framework of the Organization of American States. The Inter-American Commission for Human Rights (ICHR), chaired by Dr. Andrés Aguilar of Venezuela, received a growing number of complaints by individual Latin American citizens and international organizations. It thereby:

> decided to prepare reports on the situation on Uruguay and Paraguay, for presentation to the 7th regular session of the General Assembly of the

O.A.S. 'and also to contain those governments' in order to obtain their consent so that sub-committees of the ICHR . . . might visit those countries to gather information complementary to that already received by the Commission on the situation of human rights in each of them . . . . On March 18, the Interim Representative of Paraguay, Mr. Llanes, orally informed the acting Executive Secretary of the ICHR that his government was disposed to cooperate with the Commission in its work, but that political reasons do not recommend a visit of the ICHR at this time. On March 24, the Interim Representative of Uruguay, Dr. Araneo informed that Uruguay has ratified and ratifies its traditional pursuit and efforts in the defense of human rights but that the government cannot nor consider a visit of the Commission for the following motives: juridical reasons of national and international order, aspects tied to the national sovereignty, belief that there is no juridical merit to accept a special procedure, and for being untimely.[35]

After the period granted to Uruguay and Paraguay by the commission to accept the ICHR mission in loco elapsed, the commission requested that the reports on the situation of human rights in these two countries be included in the agenda of the next session of the OAS Assembly, which was due to convene in Grenada in June 1977. However, by a vote of eighteen to five (United States, Venezuela, Jamaica, Barbados, Trinidad and Tobago) and one abstention (Panama), it was decided against incorporating these items. This vote possibly reflects the continental picture, in which sixteen military regimes outnumber those under civilian rule. Furthermore, after a successful bout of lobbying by Uruguayan envoys, the governments of Costa Rica and Panama declined to support the original human rights motion regarding Uruguay; in the case of the latter, this occurred after Uruguayan Foreign Minister Rovira assured Panama that "Uruguay supports its rights" in regard to the canal.[36] Nevertheless, the Grenada meeting provided a framework in which a general resolution was passed against the violation of human rights, under the pretext of combating terrorism, with the support of fourteen nations, eight abstentions (Chile, Argentina, Uruguay, Brazil, Paraguay, Guatemala, Colombia, and El Salvador), and three countries absent (Bolivia, Honduras, and Nicaragua). On the other hand, at the initiative of Argentina and Uruguay, a resolution linking grants and credits of international agencies to technical considerations alone was passed, in spite of Venezuela's insistence that such aid be conditional upon the human rights situation in the recipient country.

Relations with Europe deteriorated, an important feature if one considers that it has been a major purchaser of Uruguayan goods. In 1973, the major countries importing from Uruguay had the following rank of order: Federal Republic of Germany, Spain, Italy, the Netherlands, France, United Kingdom, Brazil,

Belgium, Poland, Japan, and the United States. In 1974, the order was altered: Brazil, Federal Republic of Germany, Argentina, Soviet Union, the Netherlands, Spain, United Kingdom, United States, Israel, Greece, Belgium-Luxembourg, Chile, and France.[37]

Initially, the Soviet Union and other Communist countries decided to restrict trade with Uruguay, thereby provoking an extremely outspoken Uruguayan reaction. The Minister of the Interior, General Hugo Linares Brum (who is also closely involved with torture), accused "international Communism" of a "political and economic blockade."[38] However by 1974, following a visit by a Soviet trade delegation and the release of the former secretary general of the Uruguayan Communist party, Rodney Arismendi, the Soviets appear to have reestablished trade relations and are the fourth most important importer of Uruguayan goods (mainly wool and leather).

In 1976, Uruguay's balance of trade with the Soviet Union continued to be favorable; exporting U.S. $5,386,000 in contrast to imports of U.S. $2,636,000.[39] On the other hand, trade with Western Europe has decreased considerably. In November 1975 at a meeting of representatives of the European and Latin American parliaments in Luxembourg, which was attended by Congressman Gutiérrez Ruíz (who was later assassinated), condemnation of human rights violations in Uruguay was adopted for the first time by acclamation. This position was further developed in successive meetings of the European Parliament in January [40] and May 1977,[41] with the support of the Socialist Christian Democratic and Communist bloc. The economic ramification of such a policy was for the European Economic Community to refuse to grant Uruguay a preferential trade agreement, which had been requested by the former Uruguayan minister of economy, Dr. Vegh Villegas.

However, a sharp change in U.S. foreign policy regarding the issue of human rights in fact produced the greatest international impact on the Uruguayan regime. This process had already begun at the congressional level during the Ford administration, where liberal congressmen faced a rather hostile and conservative attitude on the part of administration. Nevertheless, amendment 502 B, granting military aid only to recipients who do not demonstrate "a pattern of gross violations of human rights" was applied to Uruguay after first being used in the Chilean case. Uruguay represented a most difficult target to hit. From the outset of the hearings, which were held in June and July 1976 at the International Organizations Subcommittee of the Committee for International Relations of the House of Representatives, Chairman Donald Fraser (Dem., Minnesota) confronted the systematic evidence of Amnesty International and Senator Ferreira Aldunate juxtaposed alongside the apologetic and fragmented answers of Deputy Assistant Secretary of State Hewson Ryan, who at great pains conceded that there were "occasional" cases of torture.[42] Representative Edward Koch (Dem., New York) then used the overwhelming evidence about human rights violations to persuade the Appropriations Committee to approve the introduction of an amendment to the foreign aid bill to cut off all military aid to Uruguay. After $7.5 million in 1976, the administration requested $3.0 million for 1977. Still, it was not yet clear that Koch's amendment would be endorsed by the two houses, and it was even more difficult to predict whether President Ford would be willing to ratify it.[43] The Latin American lobbyists (Washington Office for Latin America, WOLA; Council on Hemispheric Affairs, COHA) and human rights organizations actively mobilized support during the presidential elections to bring about the final ratification of the bill in September 1976.

Regrettably, the embassy in Montevideo did not immediately embark upon a new course of action. Ambassador Siracusa, in fact, took the decision as a personal rebuke.[44] After visiting Washington and meeting with Congressman Koch, he declared in Montevideo that the embassy and State Department were against cutting military aid to Uruguay.[45] Such a statement, contrasting what had just become official U.S. policy, could possibly have given some hope to the Uruguayan regime had Carter's election not signified that the human rights drive of the American government would be further strengthened. On February 24, 1977, Secretary of State Cyrus Vance mentioned Uruguay, together with Ethiopia and Argentina, among the countries to which military and economic aid would either be reduced or suspended. In the case of Uruguay, neither military aid nor official economic assistance ($450,000 for 1976 and $220,000 for 1977) was requested for 1978.

However, the bulk of the loans continued to flow to Uruguay through private institutions (such as the First National City Bank to which Uruguay owed 22.2 percent of its $1.158 billion foreign debt for 1976)[46] and through multilateral institutions such as the World Bank, International Monetary Fund, and Interamerican Development Bank, all controlled by the United States as a major shareholder. In 1977, the Interamerican Development Bank granted a $15 million loan to Uruguay for improving the meat-packing industry and $21.4 million for a hydroelectric project in Salto Grande.[47] The House of Representatives attempted to bridge this gap by passing a resolution instructing U.S. government representatives in international agencies to oppose extending aid and credit to those regimes grossly violating human rights,[48] but the administration resisted such a policy, considering it too extreme and preventing more flexibility and pragmatic policy.

Furthermore, the removal of Ambassador Siracusa and his retirement after thirty-five years of diplomatic service—although it could be seen as a natural course of action[49]—was accompanied by a rumor that most of his staff would be replaced in order to open a new chapter in which the embassy would cooperate with Washington's new human rights policy.

As will be discussed under the next heading dealing with perceptions, the

Uruguayan authorities reacted very sharply. Alongside Argentina, Chile, Brazil, Guatemala, and El Salvador, Uruguay was instrumental in creating a serious confrontation with the new American policy.

Reacting to Secretary of State Vance's statement threatening to suspend economic bilateral aid, following the curtailment of military assistance, the Uruguayan government condemned it as an "inadmissable act of interference in the internal affairs of Uruguay and wholeheartedly rejects it."[50]

In short, while the international community, and principally the Western nations, have become acutely aware of the repressive character of the Uruguayan regime and have started to repudiate it and even to apply economic pressure, its neighboring countries in South America, facing a similar lot, have helped Uruguay to maintain a united front.

PSYCHOLOGICAL ENVIRONMENT

At this point, it is nearly impossible to differentiate between the various proclivities among the military. Many of their policy pronouncements are ambiguously phrased, and perhaps the only vestiges left of what was once thought to be an ideological controversy is a varying dose of references to Communiques Four and Seven of February 1973.[51] Even if there are differences of opinion between Generals Cristi and Alvarez, their support is based more on personal loyalties than political ideology. It is likewise somewhat irrelevant to distinguish between the political attitudes of those civilian figures cooperating with the regime and the ruling military elite. The difference may be in quantity, the civilians being less parsimonious because of a need to publicly legitimize the reasons for their collaboration. For instance, Bordaberry, in his two lengthy secret memoranda to the military, developed the idea of doing away with popular elections in order to make the military the permanent rulers and warned against the weakness of democracy. Transitional President Demichelli managed to pass on, during his short term in office, a basic proposal for a corporativist system of representation. And finally, President Méndez has developed many interesting theories about the collapse of the traditional patterns of democracy: "Democracies have shown during these emergencies . . . incapability of the rulers to confront the disintegration of society that they themselves have helped to cause in America and is also emerging in Europe . . . rendering them incapable to solve the fundamental problems under their responsibility and assure the survival of the State."[52] Méndez's other ideas,[53] which are also disclosed in the short speeches of the military leaders, follow.

Bankruptcy of the Traditional Political Parties

The parties have become tools of subversion, instruments of Communist fronts, of corrupt parliamentary deals; they have a morally empty framework, reeking of corruption. In the future, parties must be national and not international, ''namely, not mortgaging Uruguay to the Russians or Chinese.'' Parties must be organized in such a way that they do not come between the people and the leaders. After the elections, political parties should let the authorities fulfill those promises made to the electorate, and not permanently control the members of their parties in government. With these provisions, the continuous existence of traditional political parties will be encouraged.

Legitimation of the Civil-Military Rule

The collapse of the traditional political parties and the chaos and anarchy created by subversion (Tupamaros, Communism, international parties) have justified the armed forces' entrance into politics, for it is ''the only institution found to be clean and well organized.'' Likewise, it is not dictatorial. ''The military had the strength to establish a regime which it solely ruled, but it believed that collaboration with the real forces was necessary to overcome this critical hour.''[54]

Popular Vote

At the moment, the government has legitimized itself, in the juridical and technical sense of the word, of being imposed, peacefully accepted, and being able to maintain control. One day, when it will be possible to seek the expression of the will of the people, it will be done. The system of direct and universal ballot has to be revised, as well as the electoral laws by which candidates previously were elected by a small number of voters and parties were fragilely built. Members of the armed forces will not be permitted to vote (including soldiers), in order to remove them from the passion that accompanies the struggle for political power and to guarantee that they have no personal interest or individual ambitions.

Constitutional Reform

Although the Institutional Act No. 2 of June 1976 specified that the Council of State draft a new constitution to be submitted at a later date for ''popular ratification,'' Méndez insisted that there be no constitutional reform and that some brief paragraphs become the political charter, flexible and adapted to the needs of the hour.[55]

Balance of Powers

The legislative power in the hands of the traditional and international parties has been corrupted both by its activities and lack of action that precipitated chaos. The judicial power, in spite of its excellent judges, also bore some responsibility. It was thus left to the executive power to assume responsibility and decide whether to hand over power to the dissolving forces of society or to ensure public security, with the assistance of the armed forces.

Government Priorities

There is no point now in hastening to discuss the political problems of elections that are to take place in about five years. Immediate priorities are more important than the study of constitutional reform; the economic, moral, and political recovery of the nation, and restructuring of the national economy; the transformation of the industrial structure of the country; fiscal reform; the drainage of the university; the conquest of work and obtaining security.

Human Rights

There is no reason to address such an issue when the most pressing problem is to establish order. These problems must be considered in the right perspective, for the security of the nation must prevail over human rights.[56]

As for those questions concerning the policymakers' perceptions of the internal and external environment, one can surmise from their scant references that major threats are perceived as externally based. Although references are made to the continued existence of internal subversion, even if it has in fact decreased, some have remarked that "it was defeated by the efficient action of the Armed Forces,"[57] or that "it is hard to believe that any other country but Switzerland can offer the degree of security that this government has provided its inhabitants."[58] But in all cases, there is an admission of the existence of a potential threat stemming from the link between internal and international subversion. In the words of General Vadora, "Due to the international character of subversion, the possibility of its revival is real, and therefore it is important to stress that the danger has not ended and that we still have to struggle in order to maintain the ideals of our lives."[59]

These perceptions imply that, although internal opposition is under control, "Marxist" elements abroad are now using exiles as a vehicle for anti-Uruguayan activities. As for the international community, the Uruguayan regime does not hostilely single out the Communist countries, although it sporadically refers to "Communism." While speaking about peace, peaceful coexistence and negotiations, the Communists continuously pursue their objective of destroying Western society.

However, the linkage between internal and external Communism does not confine itself only to the Soviet Union. In a virulent reaction to the curtailment of military aid by the United States, President Méndez said: "The Democratic

Party is subversion's best cohort''; he commented that Edward Kennedy ''for the sake of popularity, has now turned towards Fidel Castro, of the communist group.'' [60] In a more formal reaction, the Uruguayan government claimed that the cuts of military and economic aid ''only favor subversion and are totally inadmissible for the government and sovereignty of Uruguay.'' [61] Méndez has also branded Colombia, Peru, Ecuador, Mexico, and France as countries that will or have paid the price of giving refuge to subversion.

Reacting to the extensive reporting of the anti-American drive in the press, the military decided to restrict it. Firstly, they made sure that nothing was publicly uttered against the Pentagon. [62] Rear Admiral Márquez declared that the relations between the Uruguayan and American navies are excellent and ''are not affected by this [President Carter's] policy.'' [63] General Quirolo, when appointed military attaché to the embassy in Washington, emphasized that ''a good understanding always existed between the U.S. and Uruguayan armies.'' [64] By strengthening its relations with the military in the U.S. the regime expects to reduce the threat posed by the administration's human rights drive; in many instances, the Uruguayan generals advocated the reinforcement of intercontinental military cooperation.

Finally, the perception of a common threat helps unite Uruguay with its neighbors. ''Important countries of our continent have been shaken by the same problems. Argentina, Chile, Bolivia, Brazil, Paraguay, Peru, and Ecuador have been touched by those same social phenomena producing political repercussions and have had to abandon heterodox constitutional formulae in order to find shelter in the weapons of their armies as their only means of survival.'' [65] This image significantly helps to balance the negatively perceived image emanating from the traditional and major ally, the United States.

NOTES

1. Quoted in Oscar J. Maggiolo, ''Uruguay, Tres Años de Dictadura,'' *Nueva Sociedad* 27 (1976): 81.

2. *La Opinión*, September 22, 1976.

3. *El Día* (Montevideo), July 3, 1977, in an editorial concluding with the phrase: ''The Judicial power is dead.''

4. Interview with Senator Wilson Ferreira Aldunate, London, June 2, 1977.

5. Maggiolo, p. 80.

6. Press statement and photographs distributed by Amnesty International, London, March 1976.

7. Quoting a cable of Inter Press Service, GRISUR 66, April 20, 1977.

8. Following cables of international agencies, the head of the public relations office of the army, Colonel Luis Bertalmio, severely reprimanded the correspondents of UPI, AP, and France Press, the first two being prohibited entrance into military installations. Quoting UPI in *Semana*, Jerusalem, March 31, 1977. Apparently, twenty-five out of the fifty detained officers responsible for the memorandum were released and a communique was distributed stating that ''the arrest of the military have been discontinued because the confirmation that the recent memorandum submitted to

the upper ranks was done with the healthy purpose of rising proposals for the better development of the process that the Armed Forces are undertaking in the country and does not have any subversive character or connotation." *Boletín Informativo*, Prague, Federación de Estudiantes Universitarios del Uruguay, June 6, 1977.

9. GRISUR, 67, May 10, 1977.

10. GRISUR, 68, May 31, 1977. The text of the law is published in *El Pais*, April 22, 1977.

11. GRISUR, 66, April 20, 1977.

12. *El Día*, Mexico, June 2, 1977.

13. Amnesty International, London, NS 252/76. *Commentary on New Repressive Legislation in Uruguay, Law of "State of Dangerousness."*

14. *The Amnesty International Report 1975-6*, p. 113.

15. The *Times*, London, February 8, 1977.

16. See testimony submitted by E. Kaufman on *Human Rights in Uruguay*, Hearings before the Subcommittee on International Organizations, Committee for International Relations, House of Representatives, Washington, D.C., July 27, 1976.

17. The *Washington Post*, April 16, 1977; the *New York Times*, April 11, 1977.

18. According to a source, when Batlle was asked whether he was afraid of repercussions resulting from his critical speech on his freedom, he said that he did not believe that the military would arrest him because *they* are afraid of Jimmy Carter. GRISUR, 62, January 31, 1977.

19. *The Amnesty International Report 1975-6*, p. 113.

20. *Labor*, World Confederation of Labour, September 1975.

21. The entire text of the Decree *Ordenanza*, no. 28 was published in *El Día*, Montevideo, February 13, 1977.

22. Martin Weinstein, draft of unpublished manuscript, *Corporativism and Academic Freedom in Uruguay*, New York, 1976, p. 3. The curriculum suggests "that 'equality' is a dogma violating nature, and therefore both liberalism and Marxism are dangerous utopian positions while the 'realistic position' is founded on the acceptance of a society whose social structure reflects the 'natural order' of inequality. Presumably, this 'natural order' could include Nazism and Fascism, since the syllabus describes both as 'so-called Totalitarianisms'."

23. *Excelsior*, Mexico, June 21, 1975.

24. GRISUR, 69, June 20, 1977.

25. U.S. Department of State, *Report on Human Rights in Uruguay*, submitted to the U.S. Congress in 1977.

26. *El Día*, Montevideo, May 29, 1977, and June 2, 1977.

27. *La Mañana*, June 1, 1977.

28. *El Día*, Mexico, February 19, 1977.

29. *El País*, May 20, 1977.

30. Méndez quoted a poll of April 1977 showing that 63 percent of the population was indifferent towards political problems, while the remaining 37 percent "consists of communists, subversives and politicians who have lost their jobs." *El Día*, Montevideo, May 29, 1977.

31. See Amnesty International, *Allegations of Illicit Operations of Uruguayan Security Officials in Buenos Aires* (London, NS 215/76, September 22, 1976).

32. *Desde Uruguay*, Montevideo, May 9, 1977.

33. *El Día*, Montevideo, April 29, 1977.

34. Resolution of the Venezuelan Senate, Caracas, August 21, 1975.

35. Quoted by *Uruguayan Information Project*, Washington, April 1977.

36. *El Día*, Montevideo, June 3, 1977.

37. Data compiled by Amnesty International, *Uruguay Campaign—Foreign Trade Briefing*, London, December 1975.

38. Cable of Agence France Press, Montevideo, June 12, 1975.

39. *Excelsior*, April 22, 1977.

40. European Parliament, *Documents de seance* (Luxembourg, 544/76, January 27, 1977).

41. GRISUR, 68, May 31, 1977.

42. *Human Rights in Uruguay and Paraguay*. Hearings before the Subcommittee on International Organizations, Committee on International Relations, House of Representatives, Washington, D.C., August 4, 1976. Shortly after Ryan's contradictory testimony and attempts to cover up for the government in Montevideo, he was transferred from the State Department's second-ranking post in Latin Affairs to become its senior inspector of the U.S.-Mexican border. He has denied that the transfer was related to his testimony on Uruguay. The *Washington Post*, September 20, 1976.

43. After Ferreira's testimony on Capitol Hill, the reaction of the Uruguayan government was very severe. He was prosecuted in absence by a military court, which found him guilty of cooperation with the Tupamaros, with the immediate consequence of the confiscation of his property. Such a measure received wide publicity in the American press and indirectly affected the reaction of many congressmen who understood Ferreira paid such a price as a result of the search for true information by the Congress. It therefore helped to precipitate a critical vote against the Uruguayan regime.

44. According to Representative Koch, when Siracusa met him, "He was very upset. He was personally embarrassed that this had occurred. It make him look bad.... He had become so identified with Uruguay that it was a personal affront to him. That's the way he viewed it." *The Nation*, March 19, 1977, p. 3.

45. *El País*, October 18, 1976.

46. *International Policy Report* 3 (January 1977): 36.

47. GRISUR, 69, June 20, 1977.

48. *El País*, April 7, 1977.

49. According to the Uruguayan press, Siracusa had announced the possibility of his retirement nine months before. *El País*, April 11, 1977.

50. *El País*, March 2, 1977.

51. Statement of General Eduardo Zubia, *El País*, May 7, 1977.

52. *El País*, May 22, 1977.

53. See President Méndez's inaugural speech, *El País*, September 2, 1976, and his famous two-hour ten-minute speech in Paysandú, *El País*, May 22, 1977.

54. "The country must never relinquish the pattern of a civil-military government." Quoting a press conference of General Vadora published in GRISUR, 59, November 23, 1976.

55. "The Institutional Acts" that modify the present Constitution are going to integrate the future constitutional text." Statement by General Vadora, ibid.

56. Statement of General Vadora, *La Mañana*, May 19, 1977.

57. Statement by Foreign Minister Rovira, *El País*, May 20, 1977.

58. President Méndez's speech in Paysandú, *El País*, May 22, 1977.

59. *La Mañana*, April 16, 1977.

60. *La Mañana*, October 6, 1976.

61. *El País*, March 2, 1977.

62. *El Soldado*, Montevideo, October 9, 1976.

63. *El País*, April 29, 1977.

64. *El Día*, May 13, 1977.

65. President Méndez's speech, *El País*, May 22, 1977.

6.
Testing Hypotheses

Uruguay's civilian political tradition places it far above the Latin American average. Furthermore, as the military intervention in that country was unique, being the first in nearly seventy years, one cannot understand it as part of a recurrent pattern of behavior. Accordingly, many propositions are inapplicable (impact of border tension, cumulative effect of coup d'etat, foreign recognition, etc.). Because of the absence of such variables in our specific case; rather than challenge the validity of the general propositions, our interest is to learn from them and to examine the similarities between the Uruguayan example and those of other Latin American countries.

Most propositions present a very simple correlation between two variables, with military intervention as the independent one. One may extrapolate from the analysis itself how many internal and external factors have influenced the process. Furthermore, in many cases, there are some interfering or intervening factors that, if not introduced in the research design, might change the type of causal relationship between the dependent and the independent variables. We shall, however, limit ourselves to presenting mostly bivariate propositions as formulated by different scholars.

INTERNAL SETTING

1. "Military intervention increasingly takes the form of an attempt by the possessing classes to maintain the status quo."[1] The Uruguayan case tends to confirm the proposition. Though in the first stage it seemed that reformist tendencies were dominant, the subsequent stages confirmed the military's allegiance to the ruling classes.

2. "Military intervention is increasingly directed against legally elected

93

presidents heading constitutional regimes.'' [2] The small sample in our case does not provide a strong ground for confirmation. However, two previous cases in the 1930s and 1940s, in which the presidents behaved unconstitutionally, did not provoke any antagonistic reaction from the army; in our case, however, despite the law-abiding behavior of the president, his function in the initial phases was restricted by the army.

3. ''The overthrow of a government is more likely when economic conditions are deteriorating.'' [3] This statement is, in its broadest sense, confirmed, although one could argue that it took more than thirteen years of economic crisis in Uruguay to provoke military intervention. There is no indication as to a salient event in the economic arena that could have helped precipitate the political crisis at this particular period in Uruguayan history. However, one can look at the cumulative effect, in which the process of economic deterioration reached a level by 1972–73, facilitating military intervention. Furthermore, what was perceived by the military as bright economic prospects provided an additional incentive for intervention.

4. ''The propensity for military intervention is likely to decrease with increased social mobilization and economic development (especially industrialization).'' [4] In the past, this proposition had significantly differentiated Uruguay's civilian regime from other Latin American countries. A relative lack of increase in social mobilization and industrialization—compared with more prosperous years in the 1950s—could confirm the explanatory value of the proposition.

5. ''Military intervention is inhibited by the rise of middle strata in the social structure.'' [5] Uruguay's Colorado regime was traditionally thought to be the representative of a rising urban middle class. The Bordaberry regime represented more upper class latifundist interests and there was no direct participation of the middle class in halting the military's intervention. However, security risks and political and economic instability might have increased the middle class' passivity in accepting the imposition of a military regime. Nunn further elaborates this proposition on the basis of the Chilean experience, which witnessed a military coup against Allende in September 1973: ''Middle class size and strength is by no means a significant indicator of the military's propensity for political action. The tying of the military to class interest, moreover, smacks of Marxist, monocausal approaches to the study of civil-military relations and ignores (purposely, one may think) the fact that the military is a profession.'' [6]

In the Uruguayan case, too, it clearly appears that there is no correlation between the social class structure of the army and the type of political belief system to which it adheres.

6. ''The likelihood of military intervention is greater, the greater the cleavages and the less the consensus in a society.'' [7] This is applicable to the

Uruguayan situation, where the political polarization caused by the growth of the left produced greater divergences as to aims, as well as the presence of the urban guerrillas provoking a conflict over the legitimate means. Even among the traditional parties in Parliament, on the one hand, the cogovernmental tradition of the Colegiado period was weakened; on the other hand, particularly the Colorados and to a certain extent the Blancos were affected by a serious process of fragmentation, some of its most dynamic elements joining the left-wing Frente Amplio.

7. "Where public attachment to civilian institutions is strong, military intervention in politics will be weak . . . . The propensity for military intervention in politics decreases with increasing popular attention to and participation in politics." [8] The first part of the proposition is difficult to confirm. Although it was quite true that there was a growing disillusion with the civilian *leadership*, it does not necessarily mean that it was also accompanied by a disenchantment of the representative *institutions* of government. The second half of the proposition seems to find some basis in Uruguay judging from the diminishing participation of the public in political events, not only in favor of left-wing organizations but also when so few individuals came to the Presidential House to express solidarity in the February 1973 crisis. After the elections, it was also hard to sense an active solidarity with the traditional parties.

8. "Military intervention decreases with the increasing strength and effectiveness of political parties, of political interest groups, and of civilian governmental institutions." [9] This proposition is perhaps one of the major explanations of the factors that have affected the political process in Uruguay. Effectiveness, in whatever context it may be defined, was drastically reduced by the civilian leadership: in terms of economy, social legislation, and interest advocacy of large sectors of society, there was a general feeling of erosion in the strength of governmental institutions, while at the same time, the army projected an image of an increasingly adept force.

9. "The tendency towards military intervention increases with increasing political violence." [10] After many peaceful decades, the Tupamaros presented Uruguay with a taste of political violence and initiated the chain of reaction by which military violence was first directed against subversion, but which resulted in the violation of already weakened constitutional principles.

10. "Professionalization of the military is linked with decreased military intervention [Huntington] and with increased military intervention [Finer]." [11] Whatever the discrepancies may be about the meaning of the term "professionalization," in our case it is quite clear that Finer's view is confirmed. The organizational, technical, and professional capability—as shown in the repression of the urban guerrillas—is openly used by the military as an argument not only to justify military intervention, but to stress the patriotic contribution of this capable body to the "ruined" and "corrupted" civil administration.

11. "The 'primal claim' of the Latin American military establishment is perpetuation and security of its existence and status."[12] This feature was not emphasized in the military declaration in Uruguay. However, in their implementation and strategy, the objective of improving their social and economic status did exist. These relative gains, both as a group and as individuals, were sought through involvement in politics. The appointment of military personnel to important offices at the administrative and ministerial level (COSENA), as well as the rapid absolute and relative increase in salaries, the exemption of the military from the domestic beef ban, and the self-granting of rights to make military appointments and promotions, strongly confirm this proposition.

12. "A belief of 'Manifest Destiny of the Soldiers' is a motive disposing the military to intervene in politics."[13] Finer's excellent explanation of the feelings of patriotism and nationalism as the "moral duty" or "commitment to the people," as a genuine source of legitimization for the military, is corroborated by the analysis of the attitudinal prism of the Uruguayan generals. It is hard to assess how far this idea was manipulated by the generals as a convenient argument for justifying their aspirations for power. However, it has been confirmed by many sources that such a notion was instrumental in endorsing what apparently is a sincere involvement of the younger officers in favor of the interventionist line.

13. "All Armed Forces which become politicized as described, hold in some form or another a similar belief: that they have some special and indeed unique identification with the 'national interest'."[14] This formulation perfectly fit the repeated statements of the Uruguayan army stressing the unique character of their philosophy, which represents the *orientalidad*, namely the defense of the interests of all the Uruguayans and a refusal to be tainted as the "armed arm" of any sectoral interests.

14. "Intervention will occur when we find both disposition and opportunity to intervene."[15] Taking into account these two variables, Finer points out that the positive existence of both will produce the most likely situation for military intervention. In Uruguay this was the case. With the favorable presence of the two variables, it was possible for the military to depart from such deep-rooted traditions of noninvolvement. The weak personality of President Bordaberry and the small parliamentary support for the government gave them an ample opportunity. On the other hand, the disposition of the military to intervene was positively correlated with the increase in their antisubversive duties.

15. "The modernizing elements within the officer corps are not likely to get what they want because they are only one of the elements in most takeovers of government. Once in power, the more conservative element becomes dominant."[16] Although a few exceptions to this rule have occurred recently in some Latin American countries, this theory seems to fit the circumstances of the *autogolpe* in Uruguay. In another study of the national-reformist military

movement, Alain Rouquié presents a number of conditions for the success of such movements, and in the case of Uruguay, the more important of them are missing: extreme social and racial imbalance; the existence of disenfranchised majority sectors or severe limitations upon sovereignty; weakness of the middle class; an economy of substantial external dependency.[17]

16. "Military coups are more frequent in election years."[18] The Uruguayan example confirms this relationship. As a hypothesis with an added marginal weight, it was before Bordaberry established himself well in the government that the military rule started. The first and second crises took place during his first year in power.

17. "The strength and/or length of a country's democratic tradition some-how reduces the possibility of military 'intervention'."[19] As in the case of Chile, the military in Uruguay have helped to completely destroy this hypothe-sis. Instead, it can be argued that the lack of repeated experiences of military intervention is a contributing factor to the extremely repressive character of military intervention in countries with a deeply-rooted democratic tradition. On the other hand, one should include as an intervening factor that the above hypothesis would still be valid if threats of the extreme left, directed towards changing the traditional institutions as well as the army itself, were not per-ceived by the military. The Tupamaros in Uruguay and the Popular Unity Government in Chile could have played such a role.

18. "The apolitical tradition of a country's Armed Forces can be counted on to keep the military from covertly interfering in the political process."[20] This hypothesis is rejected by Nunn in the Chilean case. However, in observing both the processes in this country and in Uruguay, one should point out that a long road existed between the apolitical stand of the military and the actual over-throw of civilian institutions. During this extended period, "socialization" took place, providing a gradual transition between the two situations, for a period of more than two years. This, therefore, underlines the fact that the apolitical tradition could not have been changed so rapidly, and it was only after much hesitation and the purging of many constitutionalist generals that the takeover could take place.

EXTERNAL SETTING

19. "The United States military assistance is a contributing factor to mili-tary intervention[21] or does not appear to play a significant role in the proc-ess."[22] This highly disputed proposition has been thoroughly analyzed elsewhere with empirical data. Unfortunately in the case of Wolf, some of the correlations are not as valid as they previously were. Uruguay in particular fits this proposition, when in the years from 1950 to 1960, she received the highest U.S. military assistance in Latin America per capita,[23] and this was related

positively to the level of democracy. In Uruguay, as in the case of Chile (second in Wolf table, after Uruguay), the situation today is totally reversed. In our view, proving a correlation between United States military assistance and military intervention does not provide enough of an explanatory value, since there are civil governments that are loyally subservient to the United States. It is easier to prove the correlation between U.S. military assistance and dependence on the United States, with military intervention a regulating factor on deviant civilian governments. Another way of tackling this issue is to mention the existence of a third intervening value, as in the following cases of Kurth and Powers.

20. "The shift in emphasis from hemispheric security to internal security capabilities will make the Latin American military better trained and equipped than ever to intervene in the political systems of their nations." [24] This statement applies absolutely to the military role in Uruguay and might be one of the major explanations of the change. In other words, it is the previously mentioned intervening variable, "threat to internal security" (proposition 9), that explains the use of the military capability in preventing changes in the domestic structure, to the extent of entirely abolishing the civilian institutions.

21. "In the six 'semi-developed Latin American countries' (Argentina, Uruguay, Chile, Panama, Mexico, Costa Rica), the four variables of U.S. military aid, U.S. economic aid, American direct investment and American trade do not vary in ways simply and directly associated with the variation in regime." [25] This proposition was still valid when the range of deviant foreign policy behavior from one regime to another was comparatively small, and allegiance to the United States was, in different degrees, constantly maintained. Again, one must see this not only in terms of military/civilian regime, but also in terms of pro-American or anti-American orientation. In both Chile and Uruguay, when there was a change or a possible change in the pro-American orientation, the army took over. In Panama, divergence has been restrained by an expected accommodation; in the case of Argentina, the Peronist government showed signs of a rather politically independent foreign policy, with little social change in the internal structure. By now, the military regime is aligning itself with the United States. However, one must remember the military intervention when Frondizi's regime strayed from the pro-American line; in any case, the existence of exceptions to the rule does not invalidate it. One must also remember that military intervention in Uruguay came at the moment when the process of anti-American policies in South America were reaching alarming proportions. [26] Paradoxically, these variables are susceptible to change now that the U.S. Congress is making conditional some forms of aid, in particular military aid, to countries with "a pattern of gross violations of human rights." Thus in 1975 and 1976, Chile and Uruguay were excluded as recipients of military aid. As for a more general question, through an historical perspective

of the last fifty years, the concept that a higher level of development is positively correlated with a higher level of democracy still holds, although it will very much depend upon the duration of the present military regimes.

22. "The existence of a basic threat to the survival of the military institution will lead to military intervention."[27] The reference is to Fidelismo or the popular left-wing guerrilla movements, particularly during the past decade. The image of a Cuba, where the traditional army was dismantled after its defeat, seems also to have influenced the generals' decisions in countries such as Chile and Uruguay to directly intervene in the political system. This attitude of "self-defense" was clearly seen when the Tupamaros undertook a policy of attacking the military leadership as direct targets, and in many ways, precipitated the army's decision to take an active role in the country's affairs.

23. "Military intervention in one country encourages intervention by the Armed Forces of other countries in their own political systems."[28] This proposition is further developed by Fossum,[29] who differentiates between underdog neighbors, equal neighbors, and top-dog neighbors. The basic conclusion is that a neighbor effect operates only between top-dog neighbors, with a lessened interrelationship in the other cases. Applying the general proposition to Uruguay, the trend in South America of dictatorships taking over from civilian governments was in a way contagious, while the changes in regime in the immediate neighboring top-dog countries, Argentina and Brazil, influenced the regimè in Uruguay. Vice versa, after the *autogolpe* in Uruguay, the Chilean and Argentinian military coups brought about the complete disappearance of civilian regimes from the Southern Cone. The present cooperation among the military regimes of six countries (Argentina, Brazil, Chile, Uruguay, Paraguay, and Bolivia), adequately illustrates how these processes have a systematic impact.

Two additional propositions can be drawn from this study and perhaps also applied to the Chilean case, both relating to the transition from deep-rooted civilian institutions to extreme military rule.

24. "In a civil-oriented society, military takeover takes place in a gradual form rather than in the traditional way of quick coups." In other words, tactical decisions are no less important than strategic considerations. The decision to launch a coup on a particular date is not salient enough to be considered the major dividing line between involvement and noninvolvement; other prior acts should be considered as indicative of previous stages, with a high explanatory value for the understanding of the takeover.

25. "In a civil-oriented society, once started, a process of military involvement is unlikely to stop at a middle level of intervention, but will rather tend to develop to its highest and most repressive stage." A strong democratic tradition may contribute to the military's perception that anything shorter than full control and annihilation of any form of organized opposition may not succeed,

since large sectors would tend to fight back in order to reinstate the
democratically-elected institutions.

NOTES

1. Martin C. Needler, "Political Development and Military Intervention in Latin America,"
American Political Science Review 60 (1966): 619.

2. Ibid.

3. Ibid., p. 625. Johnson adds that in such cases military intervention will have popular
approval. John J. Johnson, *The Military and Society in Latin America* (California: Stanford
University Press, 1964), p. 26. We do not have enough evidence to confirm further or to elaborate
on the proposition. Putnam's interesting study, using "causal weights" or "path coefficients,"
includes the possible effect of a third variable and thereby increases the explanatory effect of the
causal analysis. Robert D. Putnam, "Towards Explaining Military Intervention in Latin American
Politics," *World Politics* 1 (1967): 83–110.

4. This and Finer's hypotheses are mentioned by Putnam, p. 85.

5. Germani and Silvert have developed such a proposition, mentioned in Putnam.

6. Frederick E. Nunn, "New Thoughts on Military Intervention in Latin American Politics: The
Chilean Case, 1973," *Journal of Latin American Studies* 7 (1974): 288–89.

7. Putnam, p. 85.

8. Samuel Finer, mentioned by Putnam, pp. 85–86.

9. Finer's and Ro. Alexander's propositions, mentioned by Putnam, p. 86.

10. E. Liewen and M. Needler came to such conclusions, quoted by Putnam, p. 86.

11. Ibid. The argument of civil supremacy in connection with professionalized armed forces is
advanced also by L.N. McAlister, "Civil-Military Relations in Latin America," *Journal of
Inter-American Studies* 3 (1961): 345–46.

12. A proposition suggested by S.E. Finer, *The Man on Horseback* (London: Pall Mall Press,
1967), p. 47. This point is well-developed in the analysis of the Argentinian situation by Marvin
Goldwert, "Dichotomies of Militarism in Argentina," *Orbis* 3 (1966): 930–39.

13. Finer, pp. 31–32.

14. Ibid., p. 35.

15. Ibid., p. 83.

16. Robert R. Adie, Guy E. Poitras, *Latin America, the Politics of Immobility* (Englewood
Cliffs, New Jersey: Prentice-Hall, 1974), p. 221.

17. Alain Rouquié, "Military Revolutions and National Independence in Latin America:
1968-1971," in *Military Rule in Latin America*, ed. Philippe C. Schmitter (Beverly Hills-London:
Sage Research Progress Series, 1973), p. 43.

18. Egil Fossum, "Factors Influencing the Occurrence of Military Coups d'etats in Latin
America," *Journal of Peace Research* 3 (1967): 234–35.

19. Nunn, p. 273. The author rejects the proposition.

20. Ibid., p. 280.

21. See Herbert L. Matthews, *Los Estados Unidos y América Latina* (México: Grijalbo, 1967);
Edwin Lieuwen, "The Military: A Revolutionary Force," in Snow, *Government and Politics in
Latin America*, p. 297; Needler, pp. 624–26.

22. Wolf, p. 890.

23. Ibid., p. 883. For the period 1962–70, Uruguay ranks third place (after Chile and Venezuela) in U.S. military assistance per soldier, and fifth per inhabitant. Figures given by Schmitter,
p. 144.

24. John Duncan Powell, "Military Assistance and Militarism in Latin America," *Western
Political Quarterly* 18 (1965): 382–92.

25. James R. Kurth, "United States Foreign Policy and Latin American Military Rule," in Schmitter, p. 310.

26. For a further elaboration on this subject, see Edy Kaufman, *The Superpowers and Their Sphere of Influence* (London: Croom Helm, 1976).

27. Goldwert, p. 938.

28. Putnam, p. 87, quoting Lieuwen.

29. Fossum, pp. 239–41.

7.
Concluding Remarks

Military intervention in Uruguayan politics has been explained in the previous chapters by a number of dependent variables from both the internal and external setting. For the most part, the findings tend to confirm prevailing hypotheses in the field, while sometimes generating others. As a whole, it seems as if it is a useful exercise to incorporate the abundant data into a methodological framework, providing a clearcut classification method together with explanatory underlying principles of the decision-making process. Brecher's framework has proved to be broad enough to be used for what apparently was an internal policy decision, namely a military coup. However, in order to provide an effective model for the Uruguayan case-study, a flexible interpretation of it is required.

First, it departs from the traditional categorization of international versus internal crisis; in the more penetrated countries, such a differentiation is misleading when considering major political and economic events.

Second, in a political setting where the traditional tripartite division of power among the executive, legislative, and judicial branches does not operate with checks and balances; furthermore, where other organized sectors of society undermine their overall political power—the definition of the "decision-making elite" has to be governed by realistic rather than formal considerations. In the case of Uruguay, the army, through the use of coercive methods, effectively eroded the basis of the legitimization of the civilian regime, and shortly after becoming involved in politics, emerged as a dominant and leading factor in the outcome of the major developments. This redefinition is thus proposed, which may also be used in the analysis of other developing countries or strongly penetrated regimes.

Third, Brecher's research outline does not include the analysis of linkages between the forces of the internal and external settings of the operational environment, a crucial aspect that should not be disregarded in countries where a prevailing foreign power not only interacts with the legitimate authorities, but expends a great deal of effort in cultivating rival forces to the government. In the case of Chile, extensive documentation has shown the relations of official and unofficial U.S. agencies and institutions (CIA, ITT, the Pentagon, AID, etc.) in establishing close ties with the military, trade unions, extreme right and left-wing organizations, student and womens' movements, etc. In the case of Uruguay, there have been no disclosures about possible covert operations of U.S. agencies during the period of our study, although some preliminary ideas may be obtained by reading Agee's chapters dealing with previous CIA activities in Uruguay.[1] In a few cases where some data were available, they have been introduced in the text not only with reference to the United States, but also regarding the dearth of practical involvement of the Soviet Union, Cuba, and China with left-wing opposition forces.

Fourth, it is difficult to provide an accurate assessment of the relative importance of the different internal and external variables in shaping political events in Uruguay. The impossibility of assigning the exact weight for each of the variables consequently precludes the ability to present the reader with an overall assessment of the forces that encourage the process of the military takeover, as opposed to those who discouraged such a trend. There is no claim by the authors of the framework of presenting such answers, thus leaving the researcher to his instinct and personal knowledge for the evaluation of causality. The absence of precise instruments, therefore, makes it necessary to speak in broad and comparative terms. Under such limitations, it is possible to state, in the case of Uruguay:

1. Internal variables seem to have played a greater role than external variables in the process of military involvement.
2. Among the external variables, the most important ones (the United States and the process in the Latin American subsystem) seem to have been perceived by the military elite as having been favorably disposed towards them.
3. As for the internal variables, the two major antagonizing forces perceived by the army elite were the Tupamaros and Congress, while the "silent majority" and the upper economic groups appear to have been perceived as positively reacting to military involvement.
4. As the military takeover was a gradual and first attempt in Uruguay's twentieth century history, it caught the party's political elite unaware of its possible consequences.

Wilson Ferreira Aldunate and the Blancos tended to direct their fire towards the civilian president. "He is the man that can get more votes in this country—as demonstrated by the last elections—and aspires that Bordaberry be dismissed in order that new elections take place."[2] Colorado member Jorge Batlle, even after being imprisoned for nearly a month by the army, stated in November 1972: "I am absolutely certain that in Uruguay a thing will not happen that did not always happen. Here there is no military power subjected to civilian power or civilian power subjected to military power. Here we are all subjected to the Constitution and law. And there are the people, who legitimize the institutional mechanisms."[3]

To complement the picture, the Frente Amplio's leader, Liber Seregni, maintained as late as June 1973 that everything seemed to point that the armed forces had no intention, in the short run, to take absolute power. "The military strategy was aimed at maintaining and emphasizing a strong incidence over the government but without assuming responsibilities for the negative aspects or deteriorating factors of government."[4]

It is worthwhile to reiterate the problems in obtaining data reflecting the opinion of the decision makers in Uruguay. In contrast to countries with a free mass media and politicians with organized constituencies, the Uruguayan military was very parsimonious and formal in its expressions; the tightly-controlled press could not help in providing informal interviews with the generals. The difficulty, then, in having a sufficient and representative data base in order to apply such methods as content analysis is somewhat compensated for by the official communiques, representing the views of the army as a corporative body.

Finally, it is hoped that this project has illustrated the importance of a multilevel analysis of political crises. Any attempt to exclusively consider internal elements, while regarding the external influences as given, fails to account for the existing linkages between domestic elements and foreign forces. Conversely, it has often been a diverting exercise to put the blame of such a crisis only on external factors and, in our case, on the presence of the predominant superpower. An analysis of the combination of the two elements must include, particularly in cases of small countries with a limited range of action, the role played by the regional setting. In the case of Uruguay, the processes that took place in the continent and the attitude of its neighboring countries created the objective conditions for the development of militarism.

It is somewhat surprising that, in spite of the extent and intensity of Uruguayan repression, which in some ways exceeded that of Chile, the Uruguayan political situation has failed to awaken even a modest level of world attention. While the coup in Chile was a one-day, dramatic event that attracted massive worldwide attention, the long and gradual process of the military takeover in Uruguay did not produce a radical turning point, nor has it created much international concern. Furthermore, the maintenance of a legal facade with a civilian president sharply contrasts with the image of the Chilean military junta. Another explanation of the world's inattention could be that for many, the role of the military in Uruguay appears to be the maintenance of law and order in a country disrupted by urban guerrillas, whereas in Chile the military abolished the legitimate government. For those who still retain the image of the *State of Siege* film as representing the situation in Montevideo, it has to be stressed that such a stage was long bypassed by the events; repression, once the Tupamaros were totally suppressed, is now aimed at any political groups which dare speak out for the reestablishment of parliamentary democracy.

In both Chile and Uruguay, each possessing a long tradition of civilian rule, liberal constitutions, and respect of human rights, the armed forces were believed to be nonpolitical. But internal strife brought about the wishful expectation that military involvement could bring back the peaceful days of the past.

Although civilian participation in governments is manifestly more prevalent in Uruguay than Chile—the president, an overwhelming majority of the ministers, and the members of the Council of State are civilians—the policies of the generals in the two countries have shown, so far, similar trends: the abolition of political parties, repression of the center and left-wing forces, a conservative socioeconomic outlook, and total identification with the United States. Recently, this last parameter has been somewhat hampered by the critical attitude of the U.S. Congress vis-à-vis the violations of human rights in the two countries; the feeling of common destiny of the two regimes has been strengthened by the decision on Capitol Hill to suspend military aid to Chile and subsequently to Uruguay.

Any predictions about the future shape of the political regime in Uruguay have to be drawn very cautiously in the context of the developments in the Latin American subsystem and possible changes in U.S. policy. The option of overthrowing the military regime through the united opposition of the center and left-wing elements in Uruguay does not seem at the moment to be a realistic proposition. Repression, though unpleasant to admit, has been successful and has totally dismantled any type of violent or peaceful organized resistance. Most of the "classic" types of dictatorships that existed prior to the guerrilla warfare in Latin America were ironically called in Spanish "*dictablanda*" (*blanda* means soft), in contrast with the present "*dictaduras*" (*dura* means hard). Systematic persecution, large numbers of political prisoners, unofficial executions, and death under torture have now related all the regimes of the Southern Cone, which maintain ties of close cooperation. Even the activities of exiled political groups in neighboring countries have been effectively curbed, keeping this part of the continent "clean" territory from any opposition to the military regime, excluding the already decreasing urban guerrillas in Argentina.

A second alternative might be the replacement of the military-sponsored president in Uruguay with a candidate elected by the traditional parties, without the interference of the army. Such a possibility could only be implemented through external pressure; important circles in the Democratic party in Congress who have special influence in the Carter administration have been conceiving of such a desired outcome. A similar strategy could apply to Chile and the eventual candidacy of former Christian Democratic President Carlos Frei.

A third possibility relates to the speculation that the army leadership itself, by internal erosion and personal disputes, would weaken its own position, a situation which would eventually lead to a transition of power to the civilian authorities. Also an element of increasing "fatigue," the natural saturation of power after a prolonged time, and particularly since the economic crisis will place a heavy burden on their function in government. Such a catastrophic prognosis of self-destruction is highly doubtful. So far, many observers have agreed that the initial outlook claiming to recognize different ideological trends among the military was grossly exaggerated.[5] With a certain historical perspective, the author must also recognize today that the tendency to overrationalize the existence of political leanings in the army had strongly influenced the first version of this study.

Thus, a nonidealized picture of the army leadership must disregard, to a great extent, divergencies in principle. Even the differences in personality and style, though occasionally felt in mini-crises, did not alter the esprit de corps of the institution in the pursuit of its governmental functions. Furthermore, the considerably rapid turnover by the usual retirement scheme of the generals, although somewhat manipulated in particular cases, guarantees a high continuity and replacement of one generation by another, still greedy for power. The decisive change will take place very shortly when the generation of the promoters of the *autogolpe* will be replaced by officers who were not in the first ranks at that time. Still, the relatively small number of the members of the military elite and the lack of specific training in many administrative fields may force the army to rely largely on civilians, which may consolidate the regime into a type of new political party with a military leadership. The likelihood of this process, rather than the dividing foreseen by the third option, reinforces a fourth possible outcome similar to the Brazilian institutional setting of a two-party system, tightly controlled and manipulated by the military. The above-mentioned plans that accompanied the installation of President Méndez seem to point to such a direction. This may well be the trend if the factors affecting the three previous options (internal opposition, the United States, and disputes among the army leadership) will not influence the present trends.

In any event, the possible return to civilian institutions will most probably be an even slower process than was the involvement of the military in Uruguayan politics. The gradual escalation to the *autogolpe* does not allow one to predict a quick return to civilian rule.

NOTES

1. Phillip Agee, *CIA Diary* (Harmondsworth, England: Penguin, 1975) and statement of CIA agent Howard Hunt, acknowledging the distribution of $100,000 a year to members of the Uruguayan government. *Desde Uruguay*, March 6, 1977.

2. *Clarín*, May 18, 1973.

3. *La Opinión*, November 28, 1972.

4. *Clarín*, June 7, 1973.

5. "The upper echelon of the Armed Forces naturally has its internal differences, but not of a doctrinaire or ideological nature, according to the unanimous opinion of the consulted observers . . . . Divergencies would then, be the fruit of clashes among personalities and styles." Ibid.

Appendix
Sequence of Events*

BACKGROUND

June 1968: Increase in Tupamaros (Movement of National Liberation, urban guerrillas), security measures increased, public liberties restricted, initiated by President Pacheco Areco.

April 1970: Foreign diplomats and expert kidnapped by Tupamaros.

August 1970: U.S. police advisor Mitrione assassinated by Tupamaros following government refusal to release guerrilla prisoners.

September 1971: Uruguayan Congress suspends habeas corpus. Increased guerrilla activity, army to lead antisubversive campaign (Decree No. 566/971).

December 1971: Formation of *"Junta de Comandantes."* For the first time, the highest-ranking officers of the three army branches organize themselves into a joint body.

End of 1971: Tupamaros declare truce, suspend guerrilla activity, wait results of left-wing front Frente Amplio in forthcoming elections.

November 28, 1971: Election results: Colorado, 41%; Blanco, 40.2%; Christian Democratic Party (Frente Amplio), 18.3%. Bordaberry replaces Areco as president.

April 1972: Bordaberry forms coalition with Colorado and Blanco participants.

April-Sept. 1972: Escalation of violence. Tupamaros prison breakout, military officers assassinated; paramilitary and right-wing forces attack left-wing centers; kill Frente Amplio militants. Joint military-police action captures most Tupamaro leaders. Guerrilla activity declines.

109

April 1972: Congress declares state of emergency (forty-five days).

May 1972: Government submits National Security Bill to Congress, asks for executive power over emergency restrictions.

May 13, 1972: Government asks indefinite extension by Congress of state of emergency (internal war). May 15: by 68 to 58, extended until June 30.

June 30, 1972: Congress extends state of emergency (internal war) 90 days.

July 18, 1972: Military accuses government officials of illegal economic activities, launches investigation into alleged activities. Defense Minister General Magnani resigns. Replaced by civilian ex-diplomat Dr. A. Legnani.

FIRST STAGE: THE OCTOBER CRISIS

September 1972: With information from imprisoned Tupamaros, army arrests dozens of people for illegal economic activity, including many connected to past and present administrations. Bordaberry establishes "Commission for the Repression of Illegal Economic Activities"—the three branches of the armed forces represented.

October 10, 1972: Five hundred officers of army and air force meet at the Centro Militar to discuss the continuation of the process of involvement, mainly against economic crimes.

October 11, 1972: Senator Zelmar Michelini (Frente Amplio) denounces detainment and torture of four physicians by conjoint military forces. Physicians released by military judge, rearrested and tortured again.

October 17, 1972: Dr. Legnani (minister of defense) demands release of doctors by military authorities.

October 18, 1972: Medical Association calls 72-hour national strike; demands doctors' release. Dr. Legnani reorders prisoners' release, consults with president.

October 19, 1972: Lt. Colonel Goldaracena disregards Dr. Legnani's order. Backed by military hierarchy in Army District No. 1 (General Cristi). President Bordaberry meets military leaders at military headquarters; minister of defense absent, uninvited. Military presents "Eight-point programme": absolute independence to "Committee for Repression of Economic Illegal Activity"; armed forces to control police; physicians continued arrest; immunity for high officers; military participation in public-owned enterprises; prevention of cattle smuggling to Brazil. Minister of defense (Legnani) and commander in chief of the army (General Gravina) resign.

October 21, 1972: Under the banner of "Law and Motherland," Senator

Ferreira Aldunate (Blanco opposition leader) calls mass protest meeting.

October 27, 1972: Senator Jorge Batlle (List "15" Colorado leader of *Unidad y Reforma*) detained. Batlle accuses the army of corruption and interference in civilian judicial investigation.

October 28, 1972: List "15" withdraws from government.

October 29, 1972: Military tribunal accuses Batlle of "an attack on the morale of the armed forces." Economic charges dropped.

October 30, 1972: Following crisis, Blanco *"Acuerdistas"* (collaborationists) increase their influence in the government. Dr. Malet new minister of defense.

November 1, 1972: Legnani letter read to Parliament by Senator Vasconcellos. Accuses military of involvement in national decision making and supervision of government.

November 20, 1972: Dr. Batlle released after threat of split in Bordaberry's coalition.

December 1972: Left wing accuses List "15" of planning to provoke clash between military and Frente Amplio in order to limit military political interests.

SECOND STAGE: THE FEBRUARY CRISIS

January 11, 1973: Army announces participation in public-owned enterprises "in merit of the personal moral capabilities, honesty, responsibility, professional and/or technical capacity that united with a high spirit of personal sacrifice in their condition as officers of the Armed Forces, makes them preferably eligible" (*La Opinión*, January 1973) for such tasks.

January 14, 1973: Government suspends three issues of left-wing newspapers.

January 15, 1973: Military vetoes civilian appointments to public-owned enterprises nominated by Batlle.

January 19, 1973: Army requests action against city council members of Montevideo for irregularities during 1971.

January 31, 1973: Colorado Senator Amílcar Vasconcellos in broadcast warns country that it is entering militaristic period.

February 2, 1973: President Bordaberry denies Vasconcellos's allegations, "as to the existence of a movement aiming [to] rule out legality, counting with the passiveness or complicity of the Armed Forces and the President of the Republic." (A. Vasconcellos, *Febrero Amargo*, Montevideo, 1973, p. 17).

February 3–7, 1973: Army chiefs request to publish answer to Vasconcellos, President denies request.

February 7, 1973: Defense Minister Mallet resigns, replaced by General

Francese. Army in unauthorized statement accuses Vasconcellos's message of being "conceived in the framework of a planned political plot aimed to strike the prestige of the Armed Forces and replace the *present* Minister of Defense Dr. A. Mallet" (my italics; the statement was published four hours after General Francese's appointment as defense minister).

February 8, 1973: Commander in Chief Martínez resigns. Army and air force barricade themselves in their bases; opposed to General Francese. Occupy television and radio stations. Navy comes out in support of government, occupies harbor and old city of Montevideo, build street barricades. Army occupies strategic positions, controls communications to capital.

February 9, 1973: Vice-President Sapelli expresses solidarity with president, repudiates that he planned to take over after Bordaberry's dismissal. After midnight, navy expresses full solidarity with legal authorities. Several hundred people demonstrate in front of presidential residence in support of Bordaberry. Three-minister committee mediates between army rebels and president. Army appoints General Hugo Chiappe Posse as "Commander of Operations for Armed Forces," usurpation of civilian right. General Francese resigns. Rear Admiral Zorrilla (head of navy) declares navy neutrality in dispute—starts to remove their street barricades. Unofficially, Bordaberry meets military demand, accepts resignation of General Francese. Army and air force publicize "Communique No. 4," political plan of nationalistic economic reforms.

February 10, 1973: Conjoint High Command (Army and air force) publicize "Communique No. 7," dealing with development and national planning, criticizing party ideologies and stressing the "myth of nationalism" or patriotism. Navy base, El Cerro, rejects authority of Rear Admiral Zorrilla, supports army statements. "Communique No. 8" announces inclusion of police force in Conjoint High Command.

February 11, 1973: Rear Admiral Zorrilla resigns, admits to "failure in inducing his subordinates to respect the basic military duty of loyalty to the Constitutional order, pride and strength of our Republic." (*Acción*, February 12, 1973) Captain Conrado Olazábal takes command of navy, adheres to "Communiques 4 and 7." Rumors of military ultimatum to president, which is confirmed at 10:00 P.M. General Chiappe Posse, Brigadier Pérez Caldas and other high-ranking officers arrive at presidential residence for meeting at 10:04 P.M.

February 12, 1973: Second meeting takes place at Boiso Lanza base. President agrees to fundamentals of "Communiques 4 and 7," stated in

"Communique No. 11." Unofficially agrees to establishment of
National Council of Security (CONASE), composed of civilians
and military, to deal with problems of security and economic
development. Refuses to lift parliamentary immunity of Senator
Vasconcellos.

February 13, 1973: New cabinet: Doctor Ravenna, minister of defense; Colonel Bollentini, minister of interior. Bollentini states: "I am a
military man, support the Armed Forces, and the way they think."
(*El Día*, March 14, 1973). Ravenna sympathizes with military
patriotism and technical capabilities. Blanco leader Ferreira criticizes Bordaberry's past refusal to initiate economic and social
reforms, skeptical of military's ability to implement such changes.

February 14, 1973: President Bordaberry broadcasts, explaining, "it was
necessary to suffer the clash of a crisis, up until now unknown to us,
in order to take full consciousness of the need for a collective effort
of all the Uruguayans . . . the Armed Forces, with great spirit and
capacity, could not remain absent and marginal" (*Cuadernos de
Marcha*, p. 41). President requests Parliament to extend for another
45 days the period of suppression of individual liberties.

February 23, 1973: COSENA (Council for National Security) officially established. COSENA's composition was: the heads of the three
branches of the armed forces; the ministers of defense, interior,
foreign affairs, and economics and Finance; the director of planning; the function of secretary of COSENA is held by the chief of
the army-police cojoint forces. (*Clarín*, February 24, 1973).

THE THIRD STAGE: THE JUNE *AUTOGOLPE*

March 23, 1973: Armed forces communique condemns illegal privileges and
special loans to congressmen. Parliamentarians accuse army of
abusing privileges.

March 26, 1973: Clash between Congress and Bordaberry. Government risks
losing parliamentary majority.

March 28, 1973: Blanco leader Ferreira declares readiness to resist threat of
military intervention.

April 1, 1973: Congress agrees to extend state of internal war for 60 days.
Reluctant to support executive inspired "Consolidation of Peace
Law."

April 9, 1973: Military demands lifting of parliamentary immunity of Senator
Erro, accusing him of maintaining links with Tupamaros. Similar
request against Senator Vasconcellos rejected by president.

April 29, 1973: Unofficial reports doubtful if Congress will achieve two-thirds
majority required to lift Senator Erro's immunity.

May 14, 1973: Troops concentrate while Congress deliberates. Armed forces make last appeal for delivering of Senator Erro to military justice. General Chiappe Posse and other officers accuse Senator Ferreira Aldunate of attempting, in February 1973, to organize a coup d'etat.

May 17, 1973: Jorge Batlle's Colorado faction announces it will aim at deposing the president if he impinges on the Constitution by bringing Erro to military justice without Senate approval.

May 20, 1973: Required two-thirds majority for Erro's submission to military justice unobtained. "Officialist" congressmen suggest "political trial" based on majority decision of two houses, and if guilty, handing him over to military justice.

June 1, 1973: President Bordaberry extends special security measures without congressional approval.

Early June: Senator Erro leaves for Argentina to participate in General Perón's presidential inauguration. Rumored he is advised to stay there.

June 15, 1973: Meeting between high-ranking generals. President Bordaberry meets General Chiappe Posse.

June 26, 1973: Rumors of presidential decision to dissolve Congress. Bordaberry meets leading ministers and then commanders of armed forces. Minister of health and education resigns, followed by three more resignations (trade and industry, public works, and budget and planning). From before midnight until 1:40 A.M. of the next day, Senate meets to condemn expected measure. Approves formation of "special investigating committee" against tortures in Paysandu district. Senate disperses. CNT declares general strike.

June 27, 1973: In early hours, army occupies Congress, led by Generals Gregorio Alvarez and Estaban Cristi. At 5:00 P.M., president broadcasts announcing dissolution of Congress, accuses them of "grave violation of the fundamental principles of the Constitution" in refusing to deliver Senator Erro to military justice. President creates Council of State appointed by himself to replace the two-house legislature; Council has mandate to draft a new constitution. Freedom of press restricted against attempts "to attribute the executive power any dictatorial purposes." Freedom of expression and public meetings forbidden. Promises to hold elections, as scheduled, in 1976. Home Affairs Minister Colonel Bollentini calls on workers to participate in new enterprise. Increases salaries to meet inflation. Following dissolution of Congress, holiday declared for primary and secondary schools. Left-wing students occupy universities.

June 28, 1973: CNT repudiates Bordaberry speech, demands: guarantee for trade unions and political activity; restoration of freedom; immediate economic measures, reestablishment of normal salary levels; and suppression of "fascist" hands.

June 29, 1973: Minister Bollentini gives trade unions ultimatum to return to work and normalize of services, refuses CNT demands. General strike continues. Communists ask for Bordaberry's resignation.

June 30, 1973: CNT outlawed, becomes clandestine organization.

July 3, 1973: Central Directive Council of the National University repudiates violation of constitutional order, and vows "to struggle against repression and barbarianism" (*La Opinión*, July 2, 1973).

July 4, 1973: Increase in salaries (insufficient to meet inflation).

July 8, 1973: Sixteen-year old Socialist militant killed by army while affixing wall posters. Fifty thousand attend funeral.

July 9, 1973: General Liber Seregni (ret.), Frente Amplio's presidential candidate arrested.

July 11, 1973: General strike collapsing. CNT officially ends it.

POST-CRISIS PERIOD

September 28, 1973: Following student death at university, government occupies campus, arrests rector and deans of most faculties.

October 27, 1973: University of Montevideo closed.

December 1, 1973: Communist party and thirteen other left-wing groups banned, including Socialist party, University National Students Federation (FEUU), Student-Worker Resistance, and others.

December 2, 1973: Government begins arresting members of the above-mentioned groups.

December 19, 1973: Council of State appointed by President Bordaberry, claiming it replaces dissolved Congress.

March 1974: All trade union activities prohibited.

May 21, 1974: Lieutenant General Hugo Chiappe Posse, a personal associate of President Bordaberry, dismissed as commander in chief of army and replaced by General Julio César Vadora, Uruguay's military attache in Washington; changes related to army dissatisfaction with performance of M. Cohen (director of central planning and interim minister of economy and finance) and Ruralist Benito Medero (minister of agriculture), who are both eventually dismissed.

July 13, 1974: New cabinet sworn in by President Bordaberry, all ministers civilians except Colonel Hugo Linares Brum, who replaces Colonel Nestor Bollentini as minister of interior.

July 27, 1974: Military takes control of major state enterprises, including central bank, oil and power monopolies, communications, and fisheries.

December 1974: Colonel R. Trabal, military attaché to France and former head of military intelligence, assassinated in Paris, allegedly by commando of the Tupamaros named Sendic, but also believed to be a result of inner purges in army ranks.

May 19–24, 1975: "Mini-crisis" between Bordaberry and General Gregorio Alvarez over economic policies when Eduardo Peile, president's friend and representative of large landowners, is dismissed as chairman of National Meat Board.

June 12, 1975: President Bordaberry visits Brazil and signs twelve agreements with President Geisel for cooperation (commercial expansion, shipping, transport, energy, hydroelectric power, etc.).

July 23–26, 1975: President Hugo Banzer of Bolivia pays state visit to Uruguay and signs four cooperation agreements.

September 17–20, 1975: President Bordaberry visits Chile, signs several cooperation agreements.

October 12, 1975: Pastoral letter signed by fifteen bishops against "hatred and violence" and for "widest possible amnesty"; its publication banned by government.

October 1975–February 1976: Several waves of arrests of members of Communist party. Estimated 700 to 1,000 imprisoned, many more escaping to Argentina and elsewhere.

December 9, 1975: First secret memorandum of President Bordaberry to military.

January 12, 1976: Ex-General Seregni, presidential candidate of the Wide Front, rearrested after being released from detention in November 1974.

February 1976: Anonymous military officer discloses in letter to the Vatican existence of terrible torture methods, illustrated by shocking photographs. Widespread international uproar.

April 21–23, 1976: President Pinochet officially visits Uruguay, ratifying number of cooperation agreements.

May 22, 1976: Congressman Héctor Gutiérrez Ruiz and Senator Zelmar Michelini's bodies found assassinated in Buenos Aires together with another Uruguayan couple, after being kidnapped on May 18. Senator Wilson Ferreira escapes murder and denounces from London the acts as perpetuated by order of the Uruguayan regime in collaboration with Argentina's security forces.

June 2, 1976: Institutional Act No. 2 requests Council of State to draft new constitution to be submitted to "popular referendum."

June 12, 1976: President Bordaberry forced to submit his resignation to military after publication of texts of two secret memoranda in which he suggested armed forces dissolve political parties, replacing them by "currents of opinion." Bordaberry would continue in office with military supervision. He is provisionally replaced by Alberto Demichelli, who held position of vice-president as head of Council of State. Interim appointment to last no more than two months.

June–July 1976: Congressional hearings on human rights in Uruguay held at the International Organizations Subcommittee of the International Relations Committee of the House of Representatives, chaired by Representative Donald Fraser.

July 6, 1976: Venezuela severs diplomatic ties with Uruguay, following incident on June 28 when Uruguayan plainclothesmen enter Venezuelan embassy in Montevideo and take away Uruguayan woman seeking asylum.

July 14, 1976: Dr. Aparicio Méndez appointed by Council of the Nation (twenty-five civilian members of the Council of State and twenty-one military of the Junta of Generals).

September 1, 1976: President Méndez takes over for five-year term. Under decree signed on day of his inauguration, all politicians (with few post factum exceptions) who stood in the 1966 and 1971 elections lose all political rights for fifteen years.

September 15, 1976: U.S. Congress decides to amend foreign aid bill, curtailing military aid to Uruguay. Later ratified by President Ford, under 502 B legislation, cutting off military aid to recipient countries demonstrating a pattern of gross violations of human rights.

October 20, 1976: At initiative of ministers of defense and interior, passage of new Institutional Act 4 the law on the "State of Dangerousness" is passed by which inclination to "Communist views" is punishable with up to six years confinement with labor though "no offence has been committed."

October 21, 1976: Institutional Act 5 restricts possibility that human rights could be protected by international organizations and justifies restrictions of "the right of Uruguayan citizens to the protection of the state as guarantee of human rights," due to existence of "subversion and terrorism."

December 24, 1976: Foreign Minister Juan Carlos Blanco replaced by Uruguayan ambassador to Israel and former minister of interior (March-November 1972) Alejandro Rovira.

Early 1977: Twenty to fifty officers arrested.

April 21, 1977: Amendment to Military Organic Laws allows for compulsory retirement of military officers, a measure that is enforced a few days later with the retirement of forty officers in the navy, allegedly supporting constitutionalist line.

June 4, 1976: Annual Congress of the Rural Federation heavily criticizes economic policies and restrictions.

June 14–22, 1977: A U.S.-sponsored motion adopted at seventh Assembly
        Meeting of the Organization of American States in Grenada, with
        opposing abstention of Uruguay, Argentina, Brazil, Chile, and
        four others.
June 27, 1977: For fourth anniversary of the *autogolpe*, Institutional Act 7
        suspends citizenship of those belonging to "political or social
        organizations that, through violence or advocating use of violence,
        tend to destroy the fundamental basis of the nation." Without
        citizenship, employment in civil service an impossibility.
June 28, 1977: President Jorge Videla of Argentina pays official visit to
        Uruguay.
July 1, 1977: Institutional Act 7 eliminates independence of judiciary power.
July 6–8, 1977: President Méndez pays official visit to Brazil.

    *The following summary is based on the Uruguayan daily press and weeklies
(*El País, El Día, Acción, El Popular, Ultima Hora, Marcha, Azul y Blanco,
Cuestión*). The subcrises periods are also covered by reports of two Argentinian
dailies (*La Opinión, Clarín*); following the establishment of total censorship in
Uruguan, other foreign sources were used such as *Le Monde* (Paris), *Keesing's
Contemporary Archives* (London), and *Facts on File* (New York).

Bibliography

BOOKS

Adie, Robert R., and Poitras, Guy E. *Latin America, The Politics of Immobility*. Englewood Cliffs, N.J.: Prentice-Hall, 1974.

Agee, Philip. *CIA Diary*. Harmondsworth, England: Penguin, 1975.

Aguilar, Alonso. *Pan-Americanism, from Monroe to the Present*. London: Modern Reader, 1968.

Alvarez, Carlos A., and Canas, Jaime E. *Tupamaros: Fracaso del Che?* Buenos Aires: Ediciones Orbes, 1969.

Amnesty International. *Annual Report 1975-6*. London, 1976.

Banales, Carlos G. "Función Política de las Fuerzas Armadas Uruguayas." In *Fuerzas Armadas. Poder y Cambio*, Luis Mercier Vega, et al., pp. 235–80. Caracas: Tiempo Nuevo, 1971.

Benvenuto, Luis, et al. *Uruguay Hoy*. Buenos Aires: Siglo XXI, 1971.

Bosch, Juan. *Pentagonism: A Substitute for Imperialism*. New York: Grove Press, 1968.

Finer, S.E. *The Man on Horseback*. London: Pall Mall Press, 1967.

Germani, Gino, and Silvert, Kalman. "Politics, Social Structure and Military Intervention in Latin America." In *Government and Politics in Latin America*, edited by Peter G. Snow, pp. 299–318. New York: Holt, Rinehard & Winston, 1967.

Grompone, A.M. *Las Clases Medias en el Uruguay*. Washington: Union Panamericana, 1960.

Guillén, Abraham. *Estrategia de la Guerrilla Urbana*. Montevideo: Manuales del Pueblo, 1966.

———. *Desafío al Pentágono, la Guerrilla Latinoamericana*. Montevideo: Andes, 1969.

Horowitz, Irving Louis. *Three Worlds of Development*, 2d ed. New York: Oxford University Press, 1972.

Instituto de Estudios Políticos para América Latina (IEPAL). *Uruguay, Un País Sin Problemas en Crisis*. Montevideo: Estudios de Actualidad, 1965.

Instituto de Ciencias Sociales. *Uruguay, Poder, Ideología y Clases Sociales*. Montevideo: 1970.

Johnson, John J. "The Emergence of the Middle Sectors." In *Latin American Politics*, edited by Robert D. Tomasek, pp. 169–97. New York: Anchor, 1966.

————. *The Military and Society in Latin America*. Stanford, Cal.: Stanford University Press, 1964.

Kaufman, Edy. *The Superpowers and Their Spheres of Influence*. London: Croom Helm, 1976.

Kissinger, Henry A. "The End of Bipolarity." In *The Theory and Practice of International Relations*, edited by F. Sonderman, W.O. Olson, and D.S. McClellan, pp. 50–54. Englewood Cliffs, N.J.: Prentice-Hall, 1970.

————. "Domestic Structure and Foreign Policy." In *International Politics and Foreign Policy*, edited by James N. Rosenau, pp. 261–75. New York: Free Press, 1969.

Kurth, James R. "The United States Foreign Policy and Latin American Military Rule." In *Military Rule in Latin America*, edited by Philippe C. Schmitter, pp. 244–314. Beverly Hills: Sage, 1973.

Labrousse, Alain. *Les Tupamaros*. Paris: Combats, Seuil, 1971.

Latin American Review of Books. *Generals and Tupamaros*. London: Latin American Newsletters, 1974.

Lieuwen, Edwin. "The Military: A Revolutionary Force." In *Government and Politics in Latin America*, edited by Peter Snow, pp. 286–99. New York, Holt, Rinehart & Winston, 1967.

Lowenthal, Abraham F., ed. *Armies and Politics in Latin America*. New York: Holmes & Meier, 1976.

Lucchini, Adalberto. *Geopolítica del Cono Sur: La Cuenca del Plata*. Buenos Aires: Juarez Editor, 1971.

Matthews, Herbert L. *Los Estados Unidos y América Latina*. México: Grijalbo, 1967.

Needler, Martin. *Political Development in Latin America: Instability, Violence and Evolutionary Change*. New York: Random House, 1968.

Quagliotti de Bellis, Bernardo. *Uruguay en el Cono Sur—Destino Geopolítico*. Buenos Aires: Tierra Nueva, Coleccion Proceso 5/6, 1976.

Rama, Carlos A. *Sociología del Uruguay*. Buenos Aires: EUDEBA, 1965.

Ramírez, Gabriel. *Las Fuerzas Armadas Uruguayas en la Crisis Continental*. Montevideo: Tierra Nueva, 1971.

Rouquie, Alain. "Military Revolutions and National Independence in Latin America: 1968–1971." In *Military Rule in Latin America*, edited by Philippe C. Schmitter, pp. 2–57. Beverly Hills: Sage, 1973.

Schilling, Paulo R. *El Nacionalismo Revolucionario* Montevideo: Ed. Diálogo, 1966.

Taylor, Philip B. *Government and Politics of Uruguay*. New Orleans: Tulane University Press, 1960.

Vasconcellos, A. *Febrero Amargo*. Montevideo: 1973.

Vemeron, Horacio L. *Estados Unidos y las Fuerzas Armadas de América Latina*. Buenos Aires: Ed. Periferia, 1971.

Weil, Thomas E., et al. *Area Handbook for Uruguay*. Washington: American University, 1971.

Weinstein, Martin. *Uruguay, the Politics of Failure*. Westport, Conn.: Greenwood Press, 1975.

Wood, David. *Armed Forces in Central and South America*. London: Adelphi Papers, 1967.

JOURNALS AND PERIODICALS

Alsina, Gerónimo. "Uruguay: la Guerra y los Tupamaros." *Revista Latinoamerican* (Bielefeld, W. Germany) 29/30 (1972):211–15.

Brecher, M., Steinberg, B., and Stein, J. "A Framework for Research on Foreign Policy Behavior." *Journal of Conflict Resolution* 13 (November 1969):75–101.

Fagen, Richard R. "The United States and Chile: Roots and Branches." *Foreign Affairs* 53 (January 1975):297–313.

Fitzgibbon, Russel H. "Components of Political Change in Latin America." *Journal of Inter-American Studies and World Affairs* 12 (April 1970): 187–204.

Fitzgibbon, Russel H., and Johnson, Kenneth F. "Measurement of Latin American Political Change." *American Political Science Review* 55 (Summer 1961): 515–26.

Fossum, Egil. "Factors Influencing the Occurrence of Military Coups d'etates in Latin America." *Journal of Peace Research* 4 (1976):228–304.

Gutiérrez Ruíz, Héctor. "Las Fuerzas Armadas y la Realidad del País." *Estrategia* (Buenos Aires) 19/20 (Nov.-Dec. 1972/Jan.-Feb. 1973):17–30.

Goldwert, Marvin, "Dichotomies of Militarism in Argentina." *Orbis* 10 (Fall 1966):930–39.

Irisity, Jorge. "Uruguay: El Francaso de la Opción Neo-liberal." *Nueva Sociedad* (San José) 22 (Jan.-Feb. 1975):17–37.

Kaufman, Edy. "La Estrategia de las Guerrillas." *Problemas Internacionales* 20 (Jan.-Feb. 1973):12–28.

Maggiolo, Oscar J. "Uruguay, Tres Años de Dictadura." *Nueva Sociedad* (San José) 27 (Nov.-Dec. 1976):74–84.

McDonald, Ronald H. "Electoral Politics and Uruguayan Political Decay." *Interamerican Economic Affairs* 26 (Summer 1972):25–45.

———. "The Rise of Military Politics in Uruguay." *Interamerican Economic Affairs* 28 (1975):32.

Needler, Martin C. "Political Development and Military Intervention in Latin America." *American Political Science Review* 66 (Summer 1966):616–27.

Nunn, Frederick E. "New Thoughts on Military Intervention in Latin American Politics: The Chilean Case, 1973." *Journal of Latin American Studies* 2 (November 1975):271–304.

Powell, John Duncan. "Military Assistance and Militarism in Latin America." *Western Political Quarterly* 18 (September 1965):382–92.

Putnam, Robert D. "Towards Explaining Military Intervention in Latin American Politics." *World Politics* 20 (October 1976):83–110.

Shapiro, Samuel. "Uruguay's Lost Paradise." *Current History* 62 (February 1972):98–104.

Wolf, Charles. "The Political Effects of Military Programs: Some Indication from Latin America." *Orbis* 8 (Winter 1965):871–93.

DAILIES, WEEKLIES, AND REGULAR PUBLICATIONS

Uruguay

Acción (daily), Montevideo.

Azul y Blanco, (weekly), Montevideo.

Cuadernos de Marcha (monthly), Montevideo.

El Día (daily), Montevideo.

El País (daily), Montevideo.

El Popular (daily), Montevideo.

La Mañana (daily), Montevideo.

Marcha (weekly), Montevideo.

Rojo Vivo (weekly), Montevideo.

Ultima Hora (daily), Montevideo.

Boletin de la Federación de Estudiantes Universitarios del Uruguay—FEUU, Prague (in exile).

Grupo de Información y Solidaridad Uruguay—GRISUR (weekly), Geneva (in exile).

Partido Por La Victoria Del Pueblo, Paris (in exile).

Servicio de Prensa de Liberación, Geneva (in exile).

Desde Uruguay, Montevideo (clandestine press).

Argentina

Clarín (daily), Buenos Aires.
Confirmado (weekly), Buenos Aires.
El Cronista Comercial (daily), Buenos Aires.
Extra (weekly), Buenos Aires.
La Nación (daily), Buenos Aires.
La Opinión (daily), Buenos Aires.

Others

Facts on File, New York.
Latin America (weekly), London.
Kessing's Contemporary Archives, London.
LADOC, Division for Latin America, United States Council of Churches.
North American Congress on Latin America—NACLA, New York.

Public Documents

U.S. Congress, House, Subcommittee on International Organizations, Committee on International Relations, *Hearings on Human Rights in Uruguay and Paraguay*, August 4, 1976. (Stenographic Transcript—Alderson Reporting, Washington, D.C.).
U.S. Congress, House, Subcommittee on International Organizations Committee on International Relations, *Hearings on Human Rights in Uruguay*, June 17, 1976 and July 27, 1976 (Stenographic Transcript—Alderson Reporting, Washington, D.C.).
Uruguay, Diario de Sesiones de la Cámara de Representantes, 609, June 22, 1972, pp. 850–78.
Uruguay, Diario de Sesiones de la Cámara de Senadores, C.S. 532, C.S. 543, C.S. 519 (1972).
Uruguay, Ministerio del Interior, Ministerio de Defensa Nacional, Publicación Oficial Conjunta, Documentos, November 24, 1973.

Unpublished Documents

Amnesty International, Commentary on New Repressive Legislation in Uruguay—*Law of "State Dangerousness,"* NS 252/76, London, 1976.
Uruguay Information Project, "Letter to Congressman Fraser," Washington, D.C., January 1977.
Weinstein, Martin, *Corporativism and Academic Freedom in Uruguay*, New York, 1977.

Index